Looking For Lizzie

THE TRUE STORY OF AN OHIO MADAM,
HER SPORTING LIFE AND HIDDEN LEGACY

Debra Lape

- Looking For Lizzie – The True Story of an Ohio Madam, Her Sporting Life and Hidden Legacy.

Copyright © 2014 by Debra Lape. All rights reserved. No part of this publication may be reproduced, stored in a retrieval system or transmitted in any form or by any means, digital, electronic, mechanical, photocopying, recording, or otherwise, or conveyed via the Internet or a website without prior written permission of the publisher; except in the case of brief quotations embodied in critical articles and reviews.

Looking4Lizzie@gmail.com

ISBN-13: 978-1492733409

ISBN-10: 1492733407

Library of Congress

Book Layout @2014 – BookDesignTemplates.com

Cover Art: by Miranda C. Peters

To Claude, Perry, Bob, Alida, and Doug for putting up with my obsession.

To Joanna for telling me that I was writing a book.

To my editor, Wendy Raymont for introducing order to disorderly Lizzie.

To Dad for being my reader, editor and enduring audience.

To Lizzie for being Lizzie.

To my mother for not being Lizzie.

Contents

A Madam in the Family 1

Farewell to All Who Knew Her 5

Sepia Ghosts 11

Next of Kin 15

Serendipitous Stow 19

Old Kentucky Home 23

On the Fast Track 29

Chicago Up in Smoke 33

Plain City Blues 37

"Dear Honey" 41

I Read It in the Papers 45

Home is Where the House Is 49

A Young Marion Daily Star 53

The White Pigeon 57

Addendum to a Presidential Legacy 61

This Bar is Closed 65

Minding the Store 69

Up to Her Pretty Neck 71

The Mayor of Akron 75

The Bigger Pond 77

Happily Ever 81

After 89

Guarding Arville 95

Mr. Dow and Mr. Winn	99
What's the Big Idea?	103
North Hill Neighbors	109
Kentucky-Grown Madams	111
Parkhursters Are Us	115
Reformer Regrets	119
Studying for the Bar	123
If It's a Girl Let's Name Her Bill	129
Familiar Terrain	133
An Orphan with the Luck of the Irish	139
Two Baptisms, One Wedding & [Almost] a Funeral	143
A Chance to Make a Mint of Money	147
We'll Leave the [Red] Light On for You	157
Someone Lit a Match in a Dry Town	161
The Little Girl Who Saw Everything	167
Gone Fishin'	173
A Spasmodic Wave of Reform	181
The Light at the End of the Tunnel is Another Train	187
Saving Those West-Enders	193
Save Yourself or Be Damned	197
Repent and Give Interviews	199
The Feathered Noose is Loose	207
Hard-Headed Romantics	213
Down On the Farm	221
Saving Lizzie	225

[Still] Looking For Lizzie	229
Curtain Calls and Walk-Ons	233
Acknowledgments	251
Methodology	253
Bibliography and Source Notes	257
Index	261
End Notes	265

PREFACE

A Madam in the Family

I'll start at the end, because that is where my search for Lizzie began. She was long dead, though I didn't know even that. I was alive and oblivious, which is as it usually is. Strangers in the same exact spot, just different time zones. My shorts and tee shirt would scandalize her. Her genteel way of trading flesh for fortune would scandalize me. We had nothing in common, except the DNA. I was standing in her daughter-in-law's bedroom in a town called Akron, the same town that she knew and loved; the same town that I know and love. We were both examining some of the artifacts of her daughter-in-law, Mattie, my great-grandmother.

There was Mattie's jewelry box of filmy crystals, tarnished sterling lapel pins and colored stones, semi-precious lapis blue with seed pearls and paste, earrings of intricately cut jade dripping like melting sherbet. Really old jewelry, unlike anything I'd seen before. It would need a great deal of cleaning and repair. So much tarnish and grime! Probably not worth the time and effort.

But that other eye on the jewelry box, the one looking over my shoulder, was seeing the jewelry as shiny-new, straight from the jewelry shop around the corner with that little bell that tinkles when you open the door, where the sales clerk in charming white shirtwaist and long black skirt is anxious to show you what just arrived from New York...

Abruptly, the magpie in me and my spare set of eyes, took hold.

There had to be more treasures in my great-grandmother's room, so my search began in earnest. There were cards, old photos, recipes, letters, old bills, journals, and in the center of the room, the single bed where she slept, her makeshift bedroom, downstairs of necessity. It was her private sanctum, a converted dining room off the living room. It was too dark to see much, and dust was now thick in the air from my intrusion. A candy tin heaped with buttons of ivory and jet winked at me, iridescently. More shiny things.

The family inheritance – a penchant for pretty jewelry.
(Great-Grandma Martha's personal collection)

Digging deep into a drawer where so many unused greeting cards and notepads were stacked, I found something odd. Pulling it out carefully, I, age 19 and from the hatless generation, did not at first recognize the object which was capped with a brilliant disk of gilded multicolored porcelain almost as big as a door knob – a hat pin of magnificent proportion, looking as if it was purchased just yesterday. Not a touch of rust or tarnish on its glinting blue foot-long length.

Somehow it had gotten stuck here in this drawer, overlooked by time itself. It was a beautiful talisman from the past, with a dangerous point. But, what *was* its point? The thing functioned like a buggy-whip in today's world. So, why did it look like new – a thing so obsolete as to become irrelevant.

Something so unimportant that she kept it until she died. So meaningless that it sits on my dresser 40 years later and I see it every day when I wake. So odd, that an old hatpin should become a touchstone to uncovering a massive cover up.

But I never look at it with just one set of eyes.

My search for the story of Great-Great-Grandmother Lizzie began in that room of dust and gemstones at the end of the life of the last descendant who knew her personally, her daughter-in-law Martha, known as Mattie.

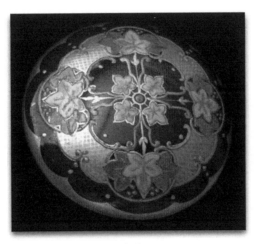

Mattie's hatpin

CHAPTER 1

Farewell to All Who Knew Her

Martha 'Mattie' Hennan Lape Atherholt [1]

Martha's son, Cleo, died nine years before her – a hard thing in the life of any parent. Harder still, because Cleo was her only child. I had never seen so many flowers and friends as graced my grandfather's funeral. Grandmother Mary, loving wife, choked back the tears, while Great-Grandmother Martha, Cleo's mother, gave way to wracking sobs. Others may believe that roses are romantic. For me, they spell funeral – that particular funeral.

Cleo's father, Arville Lape, had died decades before that, long before my father was born. Arville died before he was old enough to be called anyone's grandfather. My dad, my siblings, and I were their only living descendants. Each month, Dad would take us to visit Great-Grandma. Well into her 90's, she was still a beautiful woman with a halo of perfectly white hair. We hoped that when we grew old, we would have hair like hers. When I was a baby, she mistakenly called me "Brenda", a beautiful name that she had already bestowed, however, upon her cocker spaniel – high praise indeed for both of her special pets. She also had a little canary named Sugar that lived in a suspended silver cage, safely beyond the reach of both Brendas.

Martha's arthritic hands were paper white with dark blue-corded veins running like underground rivers. We would watch those hands lose their grip on her cane, as it slipped out of reach next to her chair. One or another of us would retrieve it and she would be content for a few minutes, until the pattern repeated itself.

The room of dust and gems was Martha's bedroom. And until she grew infirm, there was no dust at all. After her last husband Will Atherholt died, Martha took in roomers in the upstairs bedrooms. Her dining-bedroom was strategically advantageous as she could keep an eye on the comings and goings of her tenants. That mattered a lot to Martha. No hanky-panky was tolerated in her house. No guests or late hours, either. She frequently dismissed erring roomers and none too gently at that. Yes, the dining room – without doors – but with ears, was the best location for her. For privacy she had heavy velvet curtains draped at the entranceway to the living room, the kind you might see on a stage, pulled aside when the show was about to begin. She was the hard-nosed boss in her rooming house business. Her descendants thought she was a mite over-zealous in her management style. We could not have been more naive about the source of her managerial expertise.

When she became too infirm to live alone, Grandma Mary – Martha's daughter-in-law – found a comfortable retirement home for her in nearby Cuyahoga Falls, Ohio. Hers was not a voluntary exodus. As with the disappearing cane, we grandchildren often found ourselves replaying the same conversation of three minutes before. "When can I go home?" was a very sad and recurring topic.

Martha 'Mattie' Hennan Lape Atherholt   by Douglas Lape [2]

 Years later, looking back on those painfully short and final visits with Great-Grandma brought back bittersweet memories. Why didn't we ask a few standard questions such as, "What happened in the old days, Grandma?" She would probably have remembered them better than last night's dinner. Most people like to talk about their loved ones, particularly so if they are missed. We'd have been fascinated and riveted to our chairs instead of squirming in them. "How did you meet Grandpa Arville?" "When did you fall in love with him?" "Where did you live?" "What made you decide to divorce him?" "Why did you remarry him?" Yes, even then we knew that there was something unusual about Arville. Someone should have gotten the ball rolling backward in time. Martha might have opened up and told us the story of her life. Maybe even a hint or two about her mother-in-law Lizzie's life. Did these two women get along? Did Martha like her mother-in-law? Did she perhaps fill a void left when Martha's own mother died young? Just what was Martha's perspective from her late-in-life vantage point? Martha, of all the people in my family, had personally lost – and gained – more than anyone else as a direct result of the actions of Lizzie.

 Too bad we didn't know enough to start a conversation about a story buried for half a century. If only she had talked openly with her grandson (my dad) during those monthly visits. Then again, she might have believed it completely unnecessary to talk about her life. For you see, as with her confusing me with her cocker spaniel, Martha believed my dad – her grandson – was her son, Cleo. Apparently she didn't feel the need to talk to Cleo about what had happened in her life since he'd lived it, too. After a short stay at the retirement home, at age 95, Martha slipped away into that good night, taking her family secrets with her.

Sometime after Martha died, her daughter-in-law – my grandmother Mary – decided to share with us an unusual family heritage. These are the highlights of what she told us during a single conversation 37 years ago:

- One of your paternal great-grandmothers was a madam.
- She was a lady of the evening and she ran a house of ill repute in Stow Corners, Ohio.
- She came from the South.
- She had a business in Chicago and married her best customer.

That is about all I, or any of my family, can recall. My dad heard this from his mother for the first time at the same moment that she told my siblings and me. Grandma Mary probably felt that she should tell us, since there was no one else alive who knew our family history. Perhaps, she worried that it would be discovered later, and she preferred that we hear it from family.

There was much "oohing" and "ahhing" that day. Being descended from a madam had a certain cachet, so long as we were speaking of the dead and buried distant past – just an odd footnote to the family tree – really odd. Everyone wanted to ask more, but no one wanted to press the point. This was not exactly comfortable conversational terrain between a grandmother and her teenage grandchildren. The kitchen conversation was brief, and Grandma Mary herself did not seem overly certain of the long ago story.

It is possible that she did not know any other details. This was her husband's family after all, not her blood relatives. Dad didn't recall anything further, the subject having never been mentioned until then.

After 37 years this family telling had a way of twisting a bit, even with five living witnesses. For example, I recall Grandma Mary mentioning "Chicago". My dad recalls the "married her best customer" – a significant point. I do recall the overall impression that our antebellum ancestor of the evening was from the distant past, and far removed from that present day. It was apparent that Grandma Mary considered this odd personage from our line dead and buried, so why shouldn't we? She was relaying this story to us about her husband's ancestors, not *her* own. The rest of us could not say the same, as we fell into an awkward silence.

Unknowingly, Grandma Mary had released the genie from the bottle. With that awkward pause and an embarrassing change of topic, the first clues to Lizzie's story were handed to us by someone who had probably been sworn to secrecy her whole married life. The family secret was a secret no more.

CHAPTER 2

Sepia Ghosts

Our home attic had ample space to store the family photographs after Grandma Martha and Grandma Mary died. We'd viewed these photos many times, but sadly there were always people pictured in a lifetime of photographs that remained unidentified. Still, their pictures were retained along with treasured family photos. Even if they were not our family, they were *someone's* family.

While organizing and sorting in the attic one day, from one of the boxes slipped an unidentified photograph of a woman and a young girl standing beside her. Both woman and girl had dark hair. The young girl had long hair crimped in the style of that day, and very dark eyes. She wore a student's shorter dark pleated skirt and an ornately figured white blouse with epaulettes, black stockings, and a bow in her hair. The girl looked well loved and was dressed in those bows and lace mutton sleeves that were very stylish for a young girl of the period.

The woman seated next to her, leaning toward the girl, was dressed in a dark brocade flowered skirt that pooled at her feet; her high lace collar softened a bit with a pleated bodice and glinting jet jewelry. The round jet beads bubbled around her collar from which a pendant or ribbon, rested at her throat, and a long watch chain disappeared into the folds of her shirtwaist. She wore a tiny four leaf clover pinned to her blouse, reminiscent of the Four H Achievement Club, or perhaps a cross. Was she a member of some ladies relief organization of which she was justly proud to be a participant? A wedding band was visible on her left hand. Odd, that the gargoyle's head on the back of the chair aligned itself alongside that of the woman's head. Did the photographer ask the woman to lean toward the child thereby revealing the beast's flaring nostrils and furrowed brow? Or was it just happenstance? The child appeared apprehensive; the woman – serene.

She was looking directly into the camera with a semi-smile. There was no obvious wealth here, yet there was elegance in their style. They were not beautiful, these strangers, but they were striking in their dark hair and eye color. And, they resembled one another. Perhaps they were grandmother and granddaughter? There was no identification on the back of the photo[3], but it was taken in a studio, and marked Shelby, Ohio.

Shelby, Ohio meant nothing to me – no one we knew lived in Shelby. I didn't have an inkling of where Shelby was on the map, although it was less than 40

miles from where I was seated in the attic that day. I set the photograph aside and rifled through many newer snapshots and Polaroids.

The pile of family images grew. There was one of my grandfather Cleo, when he was still a youngster in Marion, Ohio. Marion – another unknown Ohio destination. The Marion photo[4] was torn in half leaving only Cleo's half. But there was someone else photographed alongside him, about his age, in a lacy dress with that long distinctively crimped hair again. Her face and most of her body were obscured, except for those tell-tale waves of hair. She had to be the girl standing next to the older woman in the earlier discovered portrait.

There was one more photo of the girl, this time reclining on a bearskin rug with her crimped hair loose all around her heart-shaped face, and her hand propping up her head. The photo was hand tinted, her young lips as red as the carpet beyond the bear skin rug. She was fully clothed right down to her shiny patent leathers. The photographer must have posed the girl, but it was not a studio photograph.

Mary Veon Jerow [5]

The backdrop looked like an old tarpaulin quickly erected for this portrait session. Maybe this photo was taken at home? Something about it was out of kilter when compared to the others. This one's subject was an innocent, but the pose seemed almost risqué. A thrill awaited me as I turned the photo over to discover the girl's name – "Mary Veon Jerow" written on the back.

"Mary Jerow was a familiar name", Dad confirmed. "Yes, Mary Jerow was probably my aunt Mary Huff". He remembered visiting Aunt Mary in Canton, Ohio and he knew that her husband's name was Floyd and her son's name was Virgil. He thought that Mary was his father Cleo's half-sister, because they grew up together.

Aunt Mary's Canton was a good place to visit back in the 30's and 40's, especially when the family traveled to the Timken Diner to feast on freshly baked pies and fried bologna sandwiches. Cleo knew Canton well. As a youth, he'd played with the Goodyear Wingfoot baseball team out of Akron and traveled to many of the parks in and around Summit and Stark Counties. I knew all this because in my attic, in the same box with the old photos, was Cleo's own photo album.

The black construction paper pages had come apart at the seams but were well captioned and bursting with Cleo's story. Not only was there the visual travelogue of the album, but also Cleo's personal journal from the period of time when he first came to Akron in 1916 after his father's tragic death.

There it was – a photo of Dad's aunt Mary with the heart-shaped face, alongside her husband Floyd and their son Virgil Huff. She was older here, but it was definitely her, in a new location – New Cumberland.

With all of this added knowledge, I wondered who then was the seated older woman with the enigmatic Mona Lisa smile? It was just a hunch, but I'd have bet my lunch that this Mona Lisa was Madam Lizzie. There was enough circumstantial evidence. Her story had been obscured and her countenance forgotten in less than three generations.

CHAPTER 3

Next of Kin

Patience is a virtue, but not if you're a genealogist. Time rapidly fills in the footprints of everyone who has gone before like so much sand on the beach. That is perhaps exactly what my family had in mind. How fast can you backfill? Yet, it can't be called buried treasure, if it were something readily known. So it is with history and its more personalized cousin – genealogy.

As a novice genealogist in the 1980's my search for Great-Great-Grandma Lizzie was stop-and-start. I wanted to find out more about her, but a family tree includes 16 great-grandmothers, and my urge was to tackle them all at once, to fill in all the missing family ancestors on all of the branches, not just Lizzie. The whole process was like a crossword puzzle. How many spaces could you fill? How fast?

I sent letters to county courthouses and likely church parishes. Genealogical research and library visits were a must. I had upward of half a dozen different library passes, tucked in my purse and ready for use, as a con man carries multiple IDs. And I talked with my family – far and away, the single best method – except in Lizzie's case, where no one would or could talk.

The first significant breakthrough on Lizzie came during the discovery of the death certificate of Arville Lape, which officially identified as his mother, one "Elizabeth Rogers" – Lizzie! My father was told that his grandpa, Arville, had died of Tetanus as a result of a motorcycle injury. Arville's heel had been caught in the back wheel of a motorcycle as he rode double and lockjaw ensued, followed by frantic attempts to stop the spreading infection by amputation. Arville's son Cleo remembers hauling away "buckets of blood" from the sick room. A gruesome memory recollected and repeated through the generations, which validated our relationship with the deceased. This was *our* Arville.

The death certificate[6] *also confirmed that Elizabeth was born in the South – just as Grandma Mary told us – in Whitley County, Kentucky. Arville's dad was listed as Jeremiah Lape, and Arville was born in Plain City, Ohio, August 17, 1878.*

Jeremiah Lape and Plain City, Ohio – these names I had seen elsewhere. Then I remembered. Following the death of my grandpa, my brother had received a box that had belonged to Cleo. It was an old walnut money box, inscribed with pencil on the inside lid:

> ***Owned By Jeremiah Lape***
> ***In 1854 Plain City O***
> ***Now owned By his***
> ***Wife Elizabeth Lape***
> ***Now Elizebeth France***

It was so grungy on the inside, my mother must have decided that her son's inheritance needed a little sprucing up, and so she lined the inside of the box with some cheery calico fabric. She outlined the pencil inscription. Her interior decorating improved it without doubt. Yes, we had found our Madam grandma. And she had a name, in fact, several names. Just how very many we would come to learn.

A Family Tree Begins to Grow

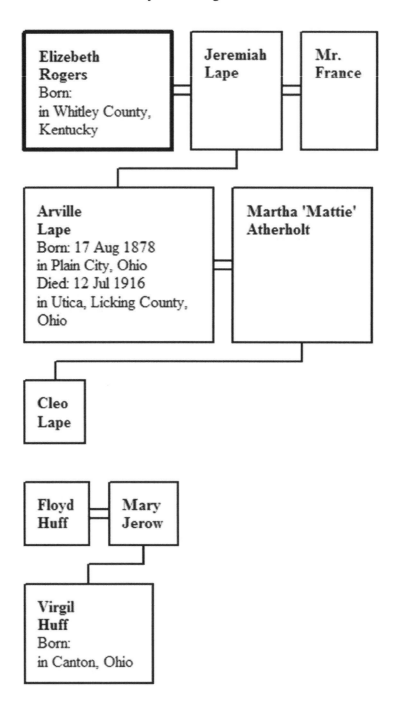

CHAPTER 4

Serendipitous Stow

During the 1980's, my husband Claude and I undertook the restoration of an 1855 farmhouse built in Wellington, Ohio. A typical form of escape during those years was a visit to an auction barn to find things that "fit" the décor. We haunted antique shops, tag sales and flea markets throughout northeast Ohio, when not building our sweat equity at the "Old Brick".

One of those jaunts took us to an early 20th century high school in Akron that had been converted into an antique mall, where each classroom had been fitted out for the different storefront tenants. One of the largest classrooms had been converted into a fabulous antiquarian bookstore. Claude found a series of used Eric Sloane books, beautifully illustrating the purpose of the various antique woodworking tools, a gift from the gods who were guiding us in our restoration.

I cruised the local history books. There was a section of lithographed pages from early atlases and directories that had been slipped into stiffening cardboard picture frames – illustrations of Cleveland, Akron, Summit County, Portage, and Stow. Stow. I remembered Stow as the place where Lizzie, under the name of Elizabeth France, had run a house of ill-repute according to Grandma Mary. I studied the Stow illustrations and found a full page illustration of a Mr. Moon's residence and, a second illustration of a building in Stow.

At that time, I didn't know much about Stow Corners, except that Lizzie had lived and worked there and, from another discovery in the attic – that my great-grandparents Martha and Arville had been married at Stow Corners, as identified on their wedding certificate – a document so coiled with age that it would not open without crumbling in my fingers.

I had a funny feeling about that lithograph, and bought it on the spot for $12 – a lot in 1984. This was one of those moments of serendipity. I knew this picture was important, but would not know how important for another 24 years.

Lithograph in hand; I visited the Fairview Park Library to see what discoveries could be made about this place called Gorge House and its owner General O. E. Gross. In 1892, Samuel Lane had the answer.[7]

1874 Summit County Atlas – lithograph of Gorge House aka Cliff House, Gen. O. E. Gross, Prop'r., Stow Corners, O.[8]

> *"CLIFF HOUSE," C. E. Kidney, Proprietor, Stow Corners. One of the most beautiful resorts for pleasure parties or private individuals, is situated near the famous glens and caves on the Cuyahoga River, in Stow Township. During the fall of 1880, Mr. Kidney purchased the "Cliff House" of Gen. Gross, and since that time has been remodeling and changing the appearance of the property, until it is now recognized as one of the leading resorts for pleasure seekers.*
>
> *This property consists of 10 acres, through which a beautiful gorge extends, and within this gorge are glens, caves and grottoes, while half a mile distant is the beautiful Silver Lake. Cuyahoga Falls is near the "Cliff House," but yet far enough distant to relieve the pleasure-seeker of the continual turmoil and bustle of the city. Around the hotel, Mr. K. is laying out walks, drives, croquet grounds, swings, dancing halls, and*

in fact has everything beautiful that will make the "Cliff House" a continuation of what it has been since coming into Mr. Kidney's hands, a grand success. Mr. Kidney was formerly a resident of Akron. He is a painter by trade, but owing to ill health he has retired from that business and engaged in his present occupation."

"Pleasure seekers", "dancing halls", "resorts for pleasure parties and private individuals" – this sounded like a very adult paradise. Although I was not familiar with the 1892 version of a subliminal message, it was there loud and clear if you were looking for it. The subject was credibly covered in such delicate terms, but the message was there alright, right between the lines.

It seemed plausible to me that Lizzie had indeed worked at this place, unless there was a pleasure palace on all four of Stow's Corners. It also seemed likely that my instinctive decision to purchase the Gorge House/Cliff House lithograph had been well founded. Who knows? Maybe it was in the genes, to like the looks of this place.

The discovery of the Stow lithograph and Arville's death certificate were personal catalysts. Lizzie seemed to be beckoning to me, to go backward into time to find her. Time travel sounds so corny, so cliché, so H. G. Wells. It didn't matter; I couldn't stop myself from continuing to look for her. Not in a hurried, rushed way, but in a "while I'm traveling near Stow / Plain City / Canton / Utica/ Whitley, Kentucky" sort of way. When opportunity arose, I didn't forget to look for her in local library stacks, cemeteries, and historical societies. Needless to say, my discoveries did not occur in the chronological order of Lizzie's life.

What follows is Lizzie's life story arranged in the order that Lizzie lived her life, not the order in which I discovered her story. And so, we will begin at the very beginning of Lizzie's life, in the South as Grandma Mary said.

CHAPTER 5

Old Kentucky Home

James Rogers, 1 of 21 Revolutionary War Veterans of Whitley County, Kentucky, Whitley County Courthouse – Williamsburg, Kentucky

In 1848, Whitley County was home to Lizzie's grandfather, James Rogers, a Revolutionary War veteran and owner of several Whitley and Laurel County properties. James was one of a handful of original settlers who along with others, helped build some of Kentucky's earliest county roads. In James Rogers' will, he excluded several of his children from any inheritance by way of leaving each of them one dollar. Prior Rogers, Lizzie's father, was one of James

Rogers' disinherited children:

> **Will of James Rogers – Excerpt**
>
> **Whitley County Will Book 1, p. 120-122 (book covers years 1818-1854)** [9]
>
> In the name of God Amen... I James Rogers Sen. of the county of Whitley and State of Kentucky being old and infirm but of sound and disposing mind and memory and wishing to dispose of my worldly estate do make and ordain this my (sic) last will and testament in the words and figures as followeth (to wit)
>
> My will and desire is that immediately after my death or as soon as convenient and the Law will permit to sell the fifty acre tract of Land I own on Laurel River at the mouth of Whipperwill creek & the money arising from the sale of the same I desire to be disposed of as follows I give one
>
> dollar to each of my sons William and John one Dollar to my son Prior One dollar to my Daughters Sally Stephinson (STINSON) one Dollar to my Daughter Rebecca Griffith and one dollar to my Daughter Mary Sexsen (SEXTON) and the residue if any to go to the payment of my Debts and lastly I hereby declare this my last will and testament hereby revoking former will or wills In witness whereof I hereunto set my hand and seal this 19th day of June 1848
>
> In presence of
> Joseph Gilliss
> Henry D. Harman

Some of James' nine children received 30 acres; other children 50 acres; some others were entrusted to care for his beloved wife Judith; still others received two cows – but not Lizzie's father Prior. The old soldier didn't provide for him.

Lizzie's granddad, James Rogers, was not only a Kentucky land-owner, but also a trail-blazer, town leader, and a soldier during his 95 years. With his will, he was passing judgment on his children from the grave, some of them painfully clear and forever known in this very public legal document. At the time of his death,

Lizzie had not yet been born. Yet James' commanding spirit was perhaps Lizzie's enduring inheritance.

If Lizzie had been a boy she might have been a soldier like her granddad who fought in the Continental Army in the Revolutionary War "Against Our Common Enemy" according to his pension application. During the Civil War years, "Against Our Common Enemy" must have confused young Lizzie no end, since her grandmother's folks were North Carolinians – Confederates. Williamsburg, Whitley County, Kentucky lay just north of the Mason-Dixon Line, so Prior Rogers was likely a Union man. Notably, Lizzie and her kin were too poor to own slaves, eliminating that conundrum.

Like many in her generation, Lizzie was a survivor of the War Between the States, spending the war in Whitley County, Kentucky. In the town of Williamsburg, where Lizzie appeared for the first and only time in the census of 1860, the roads were paved with dirt, and there were no organized churches or schools until after 1880.

Old road near Jackson, Kentucky – Marion Post Wolcott [10]

Whitley County had both Union and Confederate factions, and both are honored to this day. In neighboring Laurel County, the first battle fought on Kentucky land – the Battle of Camp Wild Cat – occurred on Oct. 21, 1861, less than one year after Lizzie's 1860 census record in Williamsburg, Kentucky. It was a Union victory.

On July 25, 1863, the war came to Williamsburg when Colonel John S. Scott arrived from Tennessee with 1,600 Confederate soldiers of the Second Cavalry Brigade, intent upon destroying Union communications, and obtaining munitions, horses, mules and cattle for the army. In Lizzie's Williamsburg, Scott was met by 100 pickets of the 44th Ohio Infantry, whom he drove back toward London, Kentucky. In the middle of the action, citizens of Williamsburg would have had property and livestock seized. One ten year old named Lizzie, might have developed a tender spot for those retreating Ohioans who were forced out of Williamsburg that day.

In much of the South, the "War Between the States" was more aptly known as the "War Amongst Us"[11]. Old Highlanders, whose ancestors stretched back to the ancient Anglo-Saxon clans of the British Isles, were on that same fence with Lizzie. The only boundary that had any real meaning for these mountain and hill folk was the hazy blue ridge that edged the perimeter of Lizzie's world. It was a fortress unto itself. It was an area of rugged beauty, but an insular cloister, too. Lizzie could count the gray wooden markers of her relatives' graves, lined up like old soldiers in the rise of the hill, back of the farm. These were the stoic soldiers that peppered Lizzie's past.

Lizzie's parents – Prior and Cynthia Rogers – had virtually nothing except for their numerous kin and children. First came oldest son J. W., then Lizzie, followed by Luke, Nancy who died in infancy, then youngest brothers Alex and Henry. They lived at the edge of town, alongside a successful boat builder named Will Sears. There was also a wealthy coal merchant family living nearby, that of Charles and Columbus Hudson. The Hudsons and Rogers families were worlds apart socially in Williamsburg. Charles Hudson owned three slaves and partner Columbus had six. The Hudson and Rogers families were not of the same social standing in Williamsburg, at one time considered the home to more coal-made millionaires than any other city in the nation.

From the Rogers' narrow door sill, Lizzie watched raw industry operate. It was a sawdust-messy, coal dust-dirty place to grow up. But for pure unvarnished energy, Lizzie and her kin were right in the middle of that action that made Williamsburg tick economically during the mid-19th century. Hardworking men and the slaves they considered chattel toiled to produce the product that fueled a nation and later, the tremendous growth of train transportation.

When James cut his son Prior out of his 1848 will, he must have had his reasons, known only to himself. A likely cause was that James considered Prior a ne'er-do-well. By age 52, Prior had not made much of himself according to the census. What was the most common cause of fecklessness, then and now?

Alcoholism. If Lizzie was part of a dysfunctional family caused by Prior's drinking and carousing, she was among a growing segment of the U.S. population. How her mother, Cynthia, handled the mess would have accounted for a lot in Lizzie's young life. Was Cynthia the fighter in the family? Did she do battle with Prior on a regular basis? Or perhaps hide the loose change from his pockets when he was snoring in his cups? Was she the pugilist in the family and the warrior of the two? Or was it the other way round? These were hard times for the Rogers family, their war years.

Nonetheless, the war between the North and the South was Lizzie's ticket to freedom. When life at the Rogers' place got even rougher and war deprivations made civilian life in Williamsburg bleaker, Lizzie surely dreamed of escaping. Accompanied by her older brother J. W., Lizzie would have watched the activities and the troop movements – the constant ebb and flow of young soldiers moving through Williamsburg – as the war progressed. Marching so straight and tall in their brilliant blue uniforms with gilded buttons, they'd have made a big impression on young hearts. And, their shiny bayonets and glinting blue steel guns would have made their own father's musket pale in comparison.

Young J. W. and Lizzie must have been thrilled by stirring stories of the soldiers, resting their horses and swapping stories outside one of the many local saloons. Were these two all ears, fascinated by the excited accounts and thrilling events of the war in distant places? Did they dare each other to get close to that Portal to Hell – that saloon door – that for all their mother's warnings – made them curious about what their father found there that made his life complete? A saloon full of handsome young soldiers would not have been the only attraction for young Lizzie. With the end of the war at hand, the traveling circuses and theater troupes that crisscrossed the country bringing live dramatic theater, resumed. There was plenty to see when these live shows arrived and set up tent at the edge of town. The circus had its wild animals, acrobats and clowns, but it would have been the singing, dancing, comedic skits and dramatic presentations that enthralled Lizzie. The actors brought Shakespearean oration to the masses. America was ready to recover, and be entertained. It was enough to make young hearts like Lizzie's beat faster. And another new development – women actors, not men dressed as women, were now among these performers. Did Lizzie's mother warn her, "Why these ladies are no more 'en prostitutes dressed up in their best clothes!" Did that matter to Lizzie at all, if she saw a way up and out and beyond those very Blue Ridge Mountains? Was this the ticket that Lizzie was waiting for, in Williamsburg, Kentucky? Or was it something else at home that made her run away. When the war ended on April 18, 1865, Lizzie was eleven and a half years old. The age of consent in Kentucky was twelve. Was she running *to* something, or running *away* from something – or someone? Run she did, burying her distant past behind her as effectively as Sherman cut his scorched earth swath through Georgia.

A Kentucky cabin in the mountains in nearby Bell County [12]

CHAPTER 6

On the Fast Track

Poverty, ignorance, abuse and neglect – some fell under these grinding wheels, while still others managed to pull themselves onto the train that carried America into the 20th century. America was a wild teenager, eagerly escaped from its pioneer swaddling clothes. And hadn't it just paid its price for freedom less than two years before Lizzie broke free of whatever constrained her in Whitley County or elsewhere?

Get on a train and go. Go anywhere and everywhere. Get out of town. Go find a new town. When Lizzie was last counted as a Whitley County resident in 1860 there were no trains, planes, or automobiles to carry her away. The L&N (Louisville & Nashville) Depot in Williamsburg would not be constructed until 1888. When Lizzie left Whitley County, she had to use the standard method of horse and wagon over the foothills of the Smoky Mountains. But everyone knew the trains were coming.

Along with the latest reconstruction reports, the newspapers were full of the new cross-country railroad developments. Land speculators were buying and selling land contracts. Town dignitaries, and the less than dignified, were doing secret deals that would affect whether their town got a place on this new high speed highway. Towns that didn't get a deal turned into ghost towns. Try finding St. Andrews, Ohio, or Cedar Mills, Kentucky, today. At least one Michigan town was double-crossed by a town official who secretly bought land in an adjacent town and lured the railroad to his new property. Yes, it was the best of times and the worst of times, with business as usual. Land speculation wasn't gambling. It was the New Economy.

To appreciate the magnitude of 19th century train capitalism, visit Biltmore in Asheville, North Carolina. In 1889 George W. Vanderbilt began construction of the largest single-family residential mansion in America, from profits earned by his father William Vanderbilt in his railroad expansion ventures.

> *Vanderbilt said in an interview with the Chicago Daily News on October 9, 1882, "The railroads are not run for the benefit of the 'dear public' — that cry is all nonsense — they are built by men who invest their money and expect to get a fair percentage on the same."* [13]

Biltmore Asheville, NC in 2010

With 250 rooms, 34 bedrooms, 43 bathrooms, and 65 fireplaces, 3 kitchens, an indoor swimming pool and 250 acres of woodland and gardens, designed by the preeminent architects of that century – Richard Morris Hunt and Frederick Law Olmsted, Biltmore is not so much a mansion as an American castle.

Young Lizzie was just a cog in the wheel of the train. More like a fly on the caboose. She must have been watching and waiting for her ticket, along with the rest of America. Destination: Chicago, Illinois.

Before, during and after the Civil War period, hard-working America loved a good show. From the lowly hurdy gurdy dancers in beer halls and saloons, to Miss Laura Keene's performance in *Our American Cousin* [14] for President and Mrs. Lincoln, America was a hungry audience. Opera houses filled with live entertainment were springing up in every self-respecting mid-size American town, but these had far less to do with legitimate opera, and far more to do with comedy routines and burlesque extravaganzas that sold well to the man on the street. In 1865 burlesque shows meant "leg shows", where the high kick was part of the feature presentation. Lizzie's was the first post-Civil War generation. She was young and lovely when America was ready to throw off its war-torn attire and become an appreciative audience. Did Lizzie hitch her ride out of Whitley County with a touring acting company? It was easy to join a traveling show as a way to get to the next bigger city. She was a performer all right, and Chicago was the biggest stage in the Midwest, packed with paying customers – the newly discharged soldiers – ready to celebrate and have fun.

Did Lizzie's acting skills drive her destiny? Probably every day of her life.[15] And according to family oral tradition, her destiny took her to Chicago, Illinois where she ran her own business. Let's call it the personal entertainment business.

CHAPTER 7

Chicago Up in Smoke

The Great Fire of Chicago Illinois, October 8, 1871 [16]

Whatever the original catalyst – abuse, poverty, greed, entrapment, liberation – Lizzie decided relatively early in her life to make a success out of a career that others would have shunned. Her migration took her from the foothills of the Smoky Mountains to the red light district of Chicago, probably the Levee, that man-made hell hole, unparalleled in the western world for its combination of prostitution, illegal activities, violence, racketeering, and unimagined cruelty and abuse by man, of man – and woman. Civilization was absent from these 20 blocks: no one was safe from the evil and foul treatment in this most inhuman zone. [17] If you were to hear a fishmonger hawking his daily fresh catch curbside, you would recognize the siren shriek of the Levee prostitutes. Some put a civilized face on it, for example, the Everleigh sisters with their gold grand piano, theatrical room décor, and doctors who made house calls to care for the "inmates"; but many lower life forms were more than willing to club a man or woman to oblivion if there was a chance to make a mint of money. There were no winners on the Levee, only hunters and their prey. The odds were stacked against the innocent. Chicago in the 1870s was a school for vice that seeded many vice-filled corners of *other* cities, as new "graduates" would leave this brothel training ground and head out for richer pastures in the west. In Chicago, Lizzie would have gotten an Ivy League education in how to be a successful madam.

Lizzie was living the low life in Chicago by the time she was 18, in business there [18] that catered to the large influx of veterans who came to the Windy City to be entertained in every sense of the word. It was a hot time in the old town, and apparently the old town was mostly made of timber. On October 8th, 1871 a scorching inferno swept over Chicago for three full days, making Hell look tame. It was the Great Chicago Fire, which was a cataclysm of biblical proportion and implication, destroying everything in its reach, as if God Himself were lighting the match to all that was evil in the man-raised city. Was it a sign that the fire burned straight through some of the worst of the evil corners of the Levee? Never mind that it took out many good neighborhoods, too.

Lizzie seemed to have taken the smoldering warning to heart. She got out of the business, temporarily at least, mending her ways by marrying her best customer, my great-great-grandfather, Jeremiah Lape.

Jeremiah Lape was a 32-year-old Union veteran. In April 1862 as a 22-year old private of Company K, 54th Ohio Volunteer Infantry (OVI) he had participated in and survived one of the bloodiest three-day battles of the war, at Shiloh, Tennessee, where he lost his sight in one eye. This was the battle that destroyed everyone's hopes for a short war. The overall number of casualties from both sides totaled nearly 24,000 soldiers – more than the battlefield casualties of the American Revolutionary War and the War of 1812, combined. Shiloh was the true beginning of the war, but for Jeremiah the soldier, the battle was over – at a horrendous personal cost. His own father Zachariah would die later as a result of war injuries.

On December 8th, 1872, slightly more than one year after the Great Fire burned out the great city of Chicago, Miss Elizabeth Rogers of Whitley County, Kentucky married Jeremiah Lape of Plain City, Ohio, in Shelbyville, Illinois.

[Marriage License image]

Jerry and Lizzie's marriage appears to have been a marriage of logical convenience between the North and the South. As my own grandmother Mary recounted to us, "She [Lizzie] was from the South." Just as Scarlett O'Hara, but by way of Chicago. First she had migrated north to Chicago, then south to Ohio. This was an unusual route for Whitley County migration, according to a volunteer at the Whitley County Genealogical & History Library in Williamsburg. "During this period, most Whitley migration occurred from east to west, not south to north."

Just two years earlier, neither Jeremiah nor Lizzie was counted in the 1870 federal census. Where they were is anyone's guess. There were many houses of ill repute counted in that Chicago, Illinois, census and if Lizzie was there by then, she was unlikely to be listed under her real name. As a wounded survivor of the Battle of Shiloh, Jeremiah might have been adrift emotionally or physically after the war, and he might have gone to visit his Lape cousins – some of whom were also Union vets – who had settled in Shelby County, Illinois. Lizzie herself had cousins living in Shelby County, too. Lizzie's aunt (James' daughter) Mary "Polly" Rogers Sexton, was four years older than Prior, and also among the disinherited. We know from their marriage certificate that by 1872, less than one year after the Chicago fire, Jeremiah and Lizzie chose this town, Shelbyville, Illinois, in which to marry. It's a reasonable guess that once married, Lizzie went with her best customer by train back to his hometown of Plain City, Ohio, to settle down and start a family.

My cousin Charlotte Kent May, grandniece to Jeremiah Lape and fellow genealogist, remembered the Plain City, Ohio, home where Jeremiah was raised, and the family as a good and hard-working people of German descent. Jeremiah's family of ten siblings was not well-to-do. Many of the boys were working at horse training and hostelry like their father who served as farrier during the war; many of the girls worked in dressmaking with their mother. The house still stands where Jeremiah's parents Zachariah and Mary Ann Lape lived on Church Street.

Church Street was separated by two small alleys from where Lizzie and Jerry rented rooms from Mrs. Almira Bigelow Thomas, a divorced and disabled woman who owned much of the block on which both Mary Ann Lape and her son, Jerry and Lizzie lived. The obvious reason they set up housekeeping there was for Jerry to aid his nearby widowed mother and youngest siblings. The other reason was because as Constable, Jerry's police station was conveniently adjacent to their rented rooms. All of Jerry's world could be found within one city block of their living space. Whatever took him to Chicago where he met Lizzie had been reconciled in his mind. He was the responsible oldest sibling of his clan, and Jerry had returned home for good.[19]

Jeremiah had hoped for a new lease on life with young Lizzie and the 1880 federal census reveals a new addition to their household – Henry Arville Lape – their new baby son had arrived in August 1878. This should have been a joyful event in the Lape household, and perhaps it was for a time.

Chapter 8

Plain City Blues

Something happened in Plain City between 1880 and 1882 that destroyed the marriage of Jerry and Lizzie. The North and the South were at war once again.

Consider the timeline:

- Lizzie and Jerry married on December 8, 1872.
- Henry 'Arville' born on August 17, 1878.
- Lizzie doing tailoring on June 2, 1880 living in rented rooms with an elderly, divorced, and land-owning woman, Almira Thomas.
- Husband Jerry was a policeman.
- Mother-in-law Mary Ann Lape died between 1880 and 1882.
- By 1882, Mrs. Lizzie Lape was boarding at Fifth Street, South of Naghten St. in the Irish neighborhood of Columbus, Ohio, just blocks from Union Station, a major train depot, 23 miles away from Plain City.

Whatever happened in Plain City, stayed in Plain City, but not Lizzie. She left town sometime after that census of June 1880, with/or without son Arville, but most certainly without husband Jerry.

Reading between the lines of the factual timeline might be helpful:

- Lizzie didn't have any children between 1872 and 1878. That's a long time between babies for that generation. Most women had babies every year, punctuated by pregnancies that failed. Perhaps Lizzie was sterile from her previous associations. Or, perhaps Jeremiah was, from his war injuries.

- In late 1877 Lizzie became pregnant. In August of 1878, Arville was born. Speculation about the birth father may have begun by Jeremiah the policeman, who knew of Lizzie's past because he was a part of it.
- Lizzie was taking in tailoring, not dressmaking. She was working with and for men in this occupation. She could easily have reestablished her prior career as prostitute or madam, making contacts and assignations between men and women.
- Jeremiah and Lizzie were boarding with an influential older neighbor named Almira Bigelow Thomas. Late in life, Almira's husband, a bar owner, ran away with a younger woman. Almira divorced him successfully, retaining her land-ownership rights subsequent to the divorce, perhaps setting a "good" example for Lizzie of how to financially survive a bad marriage with the aid of the courts. Almira died on August 15, 1880 – Lizzie's 27th birthday.
- By 1882 Lizzie had moved away from Plain City and was "boarding" in nearby Columbus close to the train depot, in a major city, and in a less than high-end neighborhood. Twenty-nine-year-old Lizzie had left 40-year-old Jerry in Plain City and headed out for greener pastures, possibly taking his money box with her. Maybe he gave it to her, maybe he did not.

Jeremiah lived another 10 years beyond the 1880 census in Plain City and was buried between his mother and father's graves. Lizzie Lape, *nee* Rogers, is not buried at Jeremiah's side, nor is she anywhere else in that cemetery.

> The G. A. R. Post here conducted the funeral of J. Lape, late of Co. K, 54th O. V. I., on Thursday last, and buried him on Sunday.
>
> L. G. Huff attended the reunion of the 54th regiment at Middletown last week. The regiment will meet here at Plain City in 1891 on the Wednesday of state fair week.

Marysville Tribune, Wed. Sept. 17, 1890 [20]

Of Jeremiah's military record, not one word was passed down to my father. If

Grandpa Cleo knew of his grandfather's service during the battle of Shiloh, no one heard it from him. It is hard to imagine that this military history would not be handed down from father to son. There were few Ohio families that did not fight in the Civil War, but perhaps their story was not looked on with honor, for the centerpiece of our story was in fact from a Mason-Dixon county of divided loyalties. Whitley County was at the very edge of the North and South.

On the other hand, maybe Cleo's father Arville wasn't Private Jeremiah Lape's son at all. Consider again, what our Grandmother Mary told us that day about Lizzie: "She married her best customer."

CHAPTER 9

"Dear Honey"

Retrieval from storage of the box of photos that belonged to Cleo was long overdue. Each time a new piece of the Lizzie puzzle was discovered, it was necessary to reexamine the big picture even if it often was simply a moment of illumination without context.

I had remembered something I'd seen in the pile of family mementos, for which I had no context. Among the box of photographs was something elegant and old and out of place. It didn't really belong to Cleo. It was too old. Cleo was born in 1898. This was an invitation to dinner – in 1882. Cleo's dad Arville was just four years old at the time of this invitation to Thanksgiving Dinner 1882 at the American Hotel in Columbus, Ohio. The note signed with a flourish on the front of the invitation read,

"Thanksgiving Day...Dear Honey – B. W. Johnson."

I had never heard this name before. Yet, the invitation was preserved along with Cleo's important papers and photographs. I did a little calculating, and

determined that Cleo's other grandmother, Alice, was alive at this time, but living nowhere near Columbus, Ohio. Plain City was just a 23-mile whistle stop to the west of Columbus. Was "Dear Honey" Lizzie?

The long-established American Hotel aka American House was in operation before, during, and after the Civil War – at a major intersection in the nation for troops and civilians. Subsequently, American House developed a seedy reputation as similarly described in Herbert Asbury's book, *Gangs of Chicago*, a story about another madam:

> *"She had come to Chicago in 1854 from Columbus, Ohio, and was chambermaid at the American House for several years, until she was seduced. Almost immediately she entered a bordello, in those days the natural and accepted sequel to a single false step."*[21]

Did such an event occur with Lizzie? In 1882? Or perhaps before she too went north to Chicago? A little more digging in the city directories unearthed more of her trail:

1882 Columbus Ohio City Directory – located about a half mile from Union Train Depot, in a predominately immigrant Irish section of Columbus:

> Lape Mrs. Lizzie, boarding, Fifth S. Naghten

1884 William's Dayton Ohio City Directory – running her own saloon adjacent to the new train station, Lizzie rented the saloon from a Mr. Clark McClung, who opened up an adjacent saloon next to hers:

> Lape Lizzie, saloon, 16 E. 6th, res same

However, by 1885 she is no longer listed in the Dayton directory, and Clark McClung has taken over her saloon location.

Plain City, 1880; Columbus, 1882; then Dayton, 1884. Was she running from Jerry? Did she take Arville with her? And why would Cleo have kept the "smoking gun" 1882 invitation from Lizzie's paramour, if that's what B. W. Johnson was? If so it may have been the straw that broke the back of his grandparent's marriage. Perhaps he didn't save the invitation at all. Maybe Lizzie saved it in the walnut box along with Arville's sporty brocade red necktie for Cleo. In the storage unit I found the necktie straight-pinned to a scrap of paper with the name "Arville", along with the gilded Thanksgiving invitation – important family mementos for which I have no direct knowledge. Yet, they clung to our family for over 100 years.

CHAPTER 10

I Read It in the Papers

In my continued searches online via Family Tree Maker and Ancestry.com, I finally hit pay dirt, and what a find! It seemed that after Dayton, Lizzie had moved on to Lima, Ohio – pronounced 'Lima' as in the bean, not the city in Peru.
Another busy train town in mid-Ohio. By 1885, Lizzie and a new husband, George Hoffman, were running a house of prostitution (full of "inmates", "Johns" and "soiled doves") and a burglary ring 73 miles from Plain City and her abandoned constable husband Jeremiah Lape. Lizzie was in jail for concealing stolen goods and was possibly involved in a mail robbery in the nearby town of Wapakoneta. The first written confirmation of the oral family history relayed 37 years ago took up two columns of the *Lima Daily Democratic Times*, April 6, 1885 edition :[22]

DAILY DEMOCRATIC TIMES,

THE LAST HAUL

Of a Gang of Burglars who have been Working This and Neighboring Towns for Several Months.

Hoffman and His Gang of Thieves and Prostitutes Finally Brought to Justice.

The Raid Saturday Night.

For the past six months our city has been being worked by thieves who carried on their plans so successfully that they escaped being caught by the police here. The "Three Johns," Smith, Doe and Beam, were caught, tried and bound over, and obtained much notoriety by escaping from our jail by way of a hole 6½x14 inches, through a stone six inches thick.

George Houzer, Marshal of Celina, arrested Mollie Silverhorn, better known here as the "Australian Girl," at Celina about ten days ago for being implicated in some petty thievings that had been going on there. She gave a description of the parties who she said were interested in it. Houzer had been over here several days before and found out that there were two parties here who tallied to the description exactly. He returned Saturday night with Sheriff Touvel, of Mercer county, and with the assistance of Marshal O'Neil and officer Berry they successfully raided the house in which they were living, and Robert Dale, Charles Burton, as they called themselves, and Mrs. Geo W. Hoffman, whose sporting name is Lizzie Lape, are now in jail. After Hoffman's arrest, the Junction House, which gained such notoriety under his management changed hands and is now a quiet and respectable boarding house. The gang then removed to a house some distance southeast of the old place. It is here that they were traced by the officers who were refused admission. Without waiting they forced the door open and went through the house. The inmates were made to get up and dress and accompany the officers. They were locked up in the city prison until last evening, when Houzer and Touviel took Dale and Burton to Celina where they are wanted for burglary. Lizzie Lape, was sent to jail for concealing stolen goods. Before they were brought down town Saturday night they were searched. Upon her person was found the watch which was stolen from the residence of W. H. Shafer, on New Years eve. The house was searched and several silk dress patterns, a half dozen silk handkerchiefs, a couple dozen silver spoons, and a large amount of cutlery was found. Several drafts and post office orders were found and it is thought that they are implicated in the mail robbery at Wapakoneta on the 23d of last month.

Slowly but surely has the case against these persons been worked. The most convicting proof against them has been discovered and will be brought against them.

The Junction House and its surroundings have undergone wonderful changes in the last few weeks. It is now in good hands and its former disreputable reputation has gone. It is now occupied by P. D. McSweeney, and is a good and respectable boarding house. The thieving gang, who met there and passed the day in shameful hilarity, while at night they executed the plans they had laid during the day, are now behind the bars, to await the beginning of the next act, when they will be called to answer for their crimes before the court of justice. Until then, at least, our city and the property of her people, are safe from the depredations of this gang.

Lizzie was not only running a prostitution ring, she was also consorting with a gang of thieves stealing silks, silver, and other shiny objects. She was a magpie, coveting trinkets. She had an eye for jewelry. She had a walnut money box of Jeremiah Lape's. Wonder if she stole that, too?

The Hoffman gang was running a notorious place called the Junction House in Lima. It was a jumping-off point for out of town travelers – a convenient location for a house of ill fame, certainly. It was apparently a common practice to locate your saloon and bordello or "house" near the tracks. Easy access, easy flight, too.

Perhaps there was more to discover about the mail robbery in Wapakoneta, but the search was in vain. The town newspapers were not yet online or were lost long ago – another dead end for now.

CHAPTER 11

Home is Where the House Is

One evening after dinner, I went to the PC to see what had arrived in the home email box: there was one newsletter message from Ancestry.com. Typically I would scan and delete it in two seconds flat. There was a blurb about historical newspapers online. I paused to read before deleting and left it in the email box for a moment longer. Returning to it later, I saw that there was a link to the historical newspapers "new content". Clicking there, I was redirected to an Ancestry website search page.

Having not previously narrowed my search to strictly historical newspapers prior to that moment, I entered Lizzie's son's name "Arville Lape", this being a fairly uncommon combination of names, unlike "Lizzie Rogers" or "Lizzie Hoffman". Here is what appeared on my screen:

ARVILLE LAPE PLEADS GUILTY TO BURGLARY

The Marion Daily Star – Feb. 6, 1902 (Marion, Ohio)

No, this couldn't be possible. The name Arville must have been more common than I had originally thought. However, it did make me uncomfortable to think that Arville might have followed in the footsteps of his mother, Madam Lizzie. If so, my great-grandfather was headliner for a bunch of burglars, rapists and shootists. Clearly, I had opened Pandora's Box.

The Marion location bothered me. Where had I seen that before? I didn't remember then, but later recalled the fractured photograph of Cleo and Mary Veon, taken in Marion. The photos were in storage now, since we'd moved away from the old farmhouse. I would have to retrieve them to discover the connection. Naturally, I didn't stop with a simple search on "Arville Lape", but backed up and narrowed my search on the Ancestry historical newspapers to include only the *Marion Daily Star*. This time I entered just the surname. Here is what showed up next:

> **Real Estate Transfers.**
>
> H. Gregory to Lizzie Lape, 1/2 acre in Marion tp., $1000.

The Marion Daily Star – April 23, 1886 [23]

A "Lizzie Lape" buying a half-acre in Marion Township for $1,000? Of husbands Jeremiah Lape or George Hoffman there was no mention at all. Here was a Lizzie Lape and an Arville Lape in the same town of Marion, Ohio, Lizzie buying land in 1886 and Arville being arrested in 1902. These dates were reasonable, relative to their ages based on the 1880 census. Arville would have been 24 when he was arrested and Lizzie would have been 33 when she bought the Marion property. The next "Lape" search hit in the *Marion Daily Star* was as follows:

> *"Lizzie Lape has purchased the house she occupies in West Marion at Sheriff's sale, paying $995 in cash for the same. Lizzie has evidently been playing to good houses, as the theatre language goes."*

Marion Weekly Star – December 24, 1886 [24]

Playing to good "houses"? What kind of theatre was this? I read, and reread this next tiny insert buried between local family holiday travel plan announcements in the Christmas edition of the *Marion Daily Star*:

> *"The talk about a public telephone office in West Marion is all bosh. The rumor has arisen from the effort of a few to have Mrs. Lape's telephone made public. This will not be done."*

The Marion Daily Star – December 25, 1886 [25]

"Public telephone office"? "Mrs. Lape's" unpublished phone number? "All bosh"? Could this be a sly little reference to the fact that Mrs. Lape was running an establishment that shouldn't be publicized? And wasn't this a form of publicity in itself? I didn't even know telephones existed in 1886! Did Mrs. Lizzie Lape have one? Was it an unlisted number? Were all of her calls routed through a telephone office with an operator? There could have been few secrets in Marion, with a population then of less than 6,000.

Everyone must have known about Madam Lizzie, including Warren G. Harding, editor of the *Marion Daily Star*, and future 29th President of the United States.

CHAPTER 12

A Young Marion Daily Star

Warren G. Harding, 1882, age 17 [26]

By late 1884, a young college grad from a nearby Ohio farm community, Warren G. Harding had moved to Marion, Ohio, along with his siblings and his homeopathic doctor parents. That fall, with the help of his father, he purchased the struggling Marion Star newspaper, and began his ascent from 19-year old editor of the Star to President of the United States. Warren was a charmer from the very beginning with many girlfriends at Iberia College. He warmed hearts among the young women and matrons of Marion, Ohio, who were always ready to be entertained at the local opera house and who enjoyed skating with Harding at the Merry-Roll-Around rink. He was a great joiner, of numerous social clubs and civic organizations, a natural people person and a town "booster" of renown. Harding had a healthy funny bone, loving all humorous diversions, including those where he could "pull someone's leg". Editor Harding was a kidder, and not much more than a kid, himself.

Harding was having the time of his young life; taking, for example, an adventurous solo train trip to the 1893 Chicago World's Fair to see the magnificent sites including the renowned snake dancer Little Egypt. Harding embraced the kaleidoscope of American life and personal freedom. He was an enthusiast. Late night soirees were the rule rather than the exception for young Editor Harding, with Marionite descendants giving accounts in as recently as 2011, of their ancestors seeing Harding returning home in the dawn hours, just as the milkman made his early morning rounds.

Harding had a true writer's gift. Once he hit his stride as editor, the Marion Star turned out humorous and entertaining accounts of life in Marion. He had an editor's skill at capturing the humility and gentle comedy in many local human interest stories in his paper. As a 21st century reader of historical newspapers, my appreciation grew for Harding's paper as compared to those of other city papers. And I read them all. He could tell a story without being judgmental, but with laughter at the shared human condition. He did not set his paper above those being reported upon.[27] He and his paper were clearly part of that ebb and flow of life, and you can tell he genuinely liked people. It is no wonder he had so many friends in high and probably low places, too.

One of Warren Harding's early editorial credos was to mention every Marionite once a year in at least one story. By that reckoning, Lizzie did remarkably well. Her business got steady coverage throughout the year. Of course, her line of work would have brought its own newspaper-selling cachet. Everyone in town and from all sides of the spectrum wanted to read stories about local crime, punishment, and redemption. Not that it made any difference to the newspaper editor. All reasons sold newspapers. For this reason alone, Lizzie got more press, in Marion and elsewhere.

Yet, Warren Harding never judged Lizzie in his newspaper. Generally, he saved that for the politicians and rival newspaper editors. Harding's paper covered Lizzie's activities with an even hand, finding more fodder among Lizzie's clients and her hired help than with Lizzie herself. In fact, beyond these earliest references to her arrival in town, her name is seldom mentioned, and with almost deference, as Harding did with all Marion businessmen. A higher caliber "house" might well have fit into Harding's enduring goal to grow Marion into a well-respected city, at least in his and Lizzie's early days in Marion. There was a shady street in Marion Ohio, and Lizzie lived and worked there, with the tacit approval of many well-respected citizens. She followed the rules of her time and profession. Warren Harding respected that.

As highest bidder for the purchase of the Marion Star newspaper, Harding benefited from a wonderful perk. John W. Dean's biography of Harding describes Harding's most valuable asset purchased that day, as an "unlimited railroad pass". Today we might equate it to a "press pass" – an invitation to go where the general public cannot – free.[28] Harding loved to travel by train to whatever destination he wished to explore. To hop a train and go to Washington to see a great orator which he did in 1892 to hear William Jennings Bryan speak, was typical of Harding.

Lizzie and Harding might have run into each other at various train stations during their travels. Would a local editor acknowledge a local madam as they both frequently rode the trains? Realistically, they shared this love of fast-moving train travel and brilliant oration with a few other million Americans.

Yet, there is a great deal of sympathy in all of the stories in Warren Harding's Marion Daily Star written about Lizzie and her full service operation. Even poetry.[29]

It was indeed a lucky Lizzie Lape who finally landed in the town of Marion, where editors and future Presidents were not only sympathetic, they also provided free promotion.

The world was a bright and shiny place for Lizzie on Christmas 1886.

CHAPTER 13

The White Pigeon

Try reading 20 years of daily newspapers for an area the width of Ohio to get a sense of the frenzied search that began in Ancestry.com's historical newspapers. I had no idea if my efforts would be in vain, or if I would continue to find more melodramatic accounts and tales of walking on the wild side with Lizzie. It didn't matter; I was hooked. Like a gold digger in the hills, I'd found a nugget, and was ready to mine the mountain. But, it was still a mountain.

Late one night, as I continued scouring the historical newspapers for accounts of Lizzie, I stumbled on a place name that was clearly associated with her – "The White Pigeon". It was, in fact the name for her operation in Marion, Ohio. From these accounts, a picture of Lizzie's business venture called the White Pigeon was starting to take shape. The historical Sanborn Insurance maps provided an excellent outline of Lizzie's Pigeon:

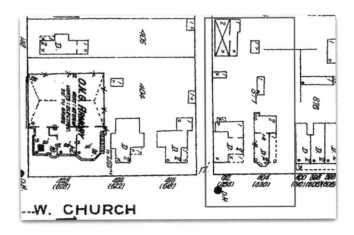

Sanborn Insurance Map 1919 [30] *– The White Pigeon Saloon marked (434) and the red house next door at (430) West Church – "The shady side of the street".*

This was the "house" that Lizzie bought in the spring of 1886 from Henry Gregory.

But what of the business name? How did "The White Pigeon" come to roost?

I looked carefully, but could find no evidence the name existed before Lizzie bought the place. Then, I stumbled on a comedic account titled "**A Lunatic Pigeon**" in the *Richwood Gazette* dated May 26, 1881.[31] Here we had the tale of a lunatic white pigeon so in love with a bottle that he made a fool of himself genuflecting and "doing homage to the bottle", "strutting round and round", "performing the most ludicrous antics", thereby losing the respect of his family and children because he longed for the bottle itself. "Sometimes this would go on for hours, the other members of his family treating his movements with the most contemptuous indifference." He succumbed in the end to his fatal attraction. I don't think we're talking root beer here. Richwood is located between Marion and Plain City. Lizzie, along with her future patrons, would have likely appreciated this bit of saloon tongue-in-cheek humor.

In 1886, while 33-year old Lizzie was working hard to make her new saloon and house, the White Pigeon, a success in Marion, young Editor Harding, age 21, with only two years under his management belt, was working equally hard to turn his fledging newspaper, the *Marion Daily Star*, around. It was tougher going for Harding. He worked tirelessly to find and edit stories that would sell papers, raise ad revenues and subscriptions, sell printing services and he personally relished the hands-on work of setting the printer's type.

These were long arduous days and nights of manning a daily newspaper – a relentless mistress. Harding did not have time for a steady girlfriend. But he apparently unwound a bit at local saloons and shady houses, according to Harding biographers. These were the days before Florence Kling entered Warren Harding's life. How Harding got to know Lizzie is not documented.

It is just possible Harding's own mother Phoebe Harding, a well-respected Marion midwife, might have had a strong opinion on which houses were more dangerous than others. Warren Harding had an abiding respect for his mother. Her opinion would have mattered to him, particularly at his age. As an active midwife, Phoebe Harding may have treated and seen these women routinely as patients. She would have known about Lizzie's business, and thus Harding would have known, too.

HOTEL MARION

MARION, OHIO.

F. G. RICHARDSON, Proprietor.

Dinner, Sunday - - - - December 6, 1885.

Vermicelli Soup.

Boiled Tongue.   Boiled Ham.   Cold Corn Beef.

Roast Loin of Beef, Brown Gravy.
Short Ribs of Beef with Brown Potatoes.
Roast Turkey, Stuffed, Cranberry Sauce.
Roast Veal.

Scalloped Oysters.
Saute of Domestic Duck.
Young Chicken Smothered, with Brown Gravy.
Apple Blanch Mange.

Southern Onions, Sliced.   Salmon Salad.   Celery.

Mashed Potatoes.   Jersey Sweet Potatoes.
Asparagus on Toast.   Rice.   Stewed Tomatoes.

Cheese.

White Bread.   Rye Bread.   Corn Bread.   Graham Bread.

Pumpkin Pie.   Apple Pie.
Cocoanut Pudding, Cream Sauce.
Vanilla Ice Cream   Assorted Cake.
Oranges.

Tea.   Coffee.

Hours of Meals.
Breakfast, 6:00 to 8:30.   Dinner, 12:00 to 1:30.   Supper, 5:00 to 7:00

Sunday Meals.
Breakfast, 8:00 to 9:00.   Dinner, 12:30 to 2:00.   Supper, 5:30 to 6:30

Star Job Printing House, Marion. O.

Warren Harding's Star Job Printing House prepared the menus for Amos Kling's Hotel Marion in 1885 [32]

CHAPTER 14

Addendum to a Presidential Legacy

Is there any evidence that Warren G. Harding and Lizzie actually *knew* each other? Or were the President and the madam just as two fast moving trains passing in the night?

Francis Russell controversial 1963 biography titled *"The Shadow of Blooming Grove – Warren G. Harding in His Times"* contains the following:

> *"From a late poker session or band rehearsal he and a few of his cronies would often slip away with surreptitious eagerness to that raw street of shaded houses near the railroad junction – Dan Fritz's White Pigeon, Annie Marie's, Lizzie Lazalere's Red House."* [33]

Young Harding was obviously part of Lizzie's story if only a visitor to the Red House. Interestingly, the gossip got it a little wrong as gossip will do. Lizzie owned the White Pigeon, while Dan Fritz ran the place for her. The Red "house" alongside the White Pigeon was always hers.

Russell's biography, though filled with fascinating facts and first-person interviews, is clouded by flagrant bigotry and dogged in its efforts to scandalize Harding. The truth is far more electric than Russell's lopsided view, and can be read through clearer lenses in *"The Presidency of Warren G. Harding"* by Eugene P. Trani, John W. Dean's biography – *"Warren G. Harding (The American Presidents Series)"* and James D. Robenalt's brilliantly researched – *"The Harding Affair – Love and Espionage during the Great War"*. A more thorough reading of Harding reveals a man who didn't need help creating scandalous opportunities. Yet, as a man-of-the-people President and good-neighbor editor, he seemed adroit at parting the waters of scandal, and avoiding the splash of mud in life that would have swamped others. He would not be as lucky in his legacy. In this, he had much in common with Lizzie.

With Russell's sources and intent in question, corroborative evidence is required to fully place Harding in Lizzie's story. Or vice versa, emphasis on vice. From Carl Sferrazza Anthony's biography – *"Florence Harding: The First Lady, The Jazz Age, and the Death of the Most Scandalous President"*:

> *"The most popular spot to find girls was John and Lizzie Lazalere's Red Bird Saloon, near the railroad tracks. That Warren knew it well was indicated in an early edition of the Star when after luring a newspaper rival there, he staged a fake raid and the next day made barnyard allusions to it in his paper."* [34]

The 22-year old Warren and Lizzie, 34, were both relative newcomers to Marion, Ohio, and outsiders at that, in the spring of 1887. In 1885 when Lizzie first arrived in Marion and purchased the White Pigeon and adjacent Red "house", she was a worldly woman with a clear vision of what she wanted out of life. She'd done the unthinkable and succeeded. She was "playing to a good house" as the newspaper put it. Editor Harding, from a rural background, would have been impressed with Lizzie's Chicago polish. Lizzie had the best girls, the best buffet, the best poker games, the best source of ribald stories, and the best place to engineer a genuinely naughty practical joke on a newspaper competitor and old friend, Colonel James Vaughan.

Beneath the surface, Warren and Lizzie were train-track sophisticates. Warren had parents who were working doctors – not considered Marion's elite. Lizzie herself was an entirely self-made woman. Her independence was more like an emancipation – a burst of freedom made sweeter when contrasted with her bitter existence in Chicago or earlier during the war years.

She'd fashioned herself into the Lizzie that Marion knew – a determined, entertaining, and imaginative woman of means. Her businesses were the "in" places where grownups wanting to walk on the wild side, gathered. Warren Harding was one of those.

What was it like, that night when Harding staged his fake police raid at her "Red Manse" and Colonel Vaughan was so unceremoniously seized? Who did he enlist to play police? Were all the girls and staff in on the joke? What was the ruse that Harding used to lure the unsuspecting Colonel? And did the Colonel, editor Vaughan of the rival *Daily Mirror*, expect to find a story, and instead discover that he himself was the butt of the joke?

Lizzie and Warren had to be in cahoots for this fake raid to succeed. To have organized it without Lizzie knowing would have been to make an enemy of the owner of the place where a younger Warren liked to hang his hat for an evening's entertainment.

Harding's joke backfired on the editor prankster. Colonel Vaughan, his old employer and family friend, never forgave Warren for the embarrassment at Lizzie's. In impulsive retaliation, Vaughan unleashed the shadow of bigotry on his competitor in publishing and politics. Vaughan had drafted in his newspaper the *Marion Mirror*, a broadside aimed at Harding's rumored black ancestry. Having second thoughts, Vaughan then destroyed all copies before they were released. The fact that Vaughan, a Harding family friend, would even consider publishing such an inflammatory story, lent credence to the bigotry.

Harding was aware of Vaughan's anger at the prank-gone-wrong and published this cryptic apology in the *Star*:

> *"The humor that Vaughan misses – that grand old, elegant gentleman who edits the Mirror – is of little consequence. Jim never fails to inquire, if the chicken coop is locked."*

Marion Daily Star – May 11, 1887

At the time, Harding was a 21 year-old. His practical joke at Lizzie's had created a racial maelstrom that would matter much to those that judged him and his legacy. Harding may have been a self-described *bloviator*, but he did not bend to the bigots, refusing to provide scandal mongers any denial of the racial accusations.

Perhaps this early personal exposure to racism helped shape Harding's presidency. In 1921, President Harding would travel to Birmingham, Alabama to give a speech supporting the anti-lynching bill pending in Congress. It was one of the earliest civil rights movement speeches given in the Deep South.

That evening's prank at the White Pigeon and its repercussions would long be remembered by Harding and Lizzie.

Chapter 15

This Bar is Closed

Sometime between 1887 and 1890, Lizzie decided to expand her enterprise to multiple locations. Perhaps the White Pigeon wasn't achieving the success in Marion she had experienced in Chicago prior to the Great Fire. Or maybe it was so successful she felt it could be replicated elsewhere. Then again, maybe she was simply repeating the pattern of her previous flights; she could do bigger and better than Marion. Akron, a full-fledged city, unlike little Marion, was Lizzie's next destination and she had in tow a brand new husband – number three – John "Jack" Larzelere from Muskingum, Ohio. No sign of husband number two, George W. Hoffman, or clue as to how she ditched him. Hoffman disappeared off the Lizzie research trail as fast as he had arrived. I could not prove with marriage or divorce record if they were actually married, unlike the rest of Lizzie's husbands.

Just who was Jack Larzelere? And what do we know about Jack beyond his wonderfully alliterative surname? "Lizzie Larzelere" has a nice ring to it – a name with three zzz's and as many lll's.

Jack's name first appears in print in *The Marion Star* in 1886. He was working as saloon keeper at the old Kerr House Hotel, not far from Amos Kling's new Marion Hotel. Kling was the very rich, very hard-hearted banker father of Florence, future wife of President Warren Harding. That same year, Florence divorced her first husband Henry "Pete" DeWolfe. Pete had a drinking problem and had deserted Florence in 1880, just months after she gave birth to their only son Marshall. Penniless and destitute, she returned to Marion with her baby and was not allowed back into her father's home until she agreed to give up custody of her son to her father.

In December 1886, Jack Larzelere was arrested for serving liquor to a "person in the habit of getting drunk" – none other than Amos Kling's former son-in-law, Henry "Pete" DeWolfe:

> **Arrested for Selling Intoxicants.**
>
> The persons who sold Henry DeWolfe liquor Friday evening were arrested Saturday afternoon... State of Ohio vs. John E. Lazalere and John Doe. Information charging them with selling intoxicating liquors to a person in the habit of getting drunk. Both have bonds for their appearance in court of $200 each.

Marion Daily Star – Dec. 11, 1886 [35]

Amos Kling, a vindictive man, may have had something to do with pressing charges against Jack Larzelere. Kling no doubt thoroughly disliked his drunken ex-son-in-law and the proximity of the offense to his reputable Marion Hotel, the fact that the event occurred in a competing establishment, and the bad press given him by Warren G. Harding's *Marion Daily Star*. Ultra-conservative Marion businessman Kling's dislike of young editor Harding grew into open hatred when Harding began courting Kling's daughter, Florence Kling DeWolfe and married her on July 8, 1891.

No doubt Jack Larzelere had an inkling of the political and financial mess he'd landed in, for the next story appearing in the Feb. 17, 1887, *Marion Star* indicated he had decided to pull up stakes and was leaving town for greener pastures.

> "Jack Lazalere has sold the Kerr House saloon and intends leaving Marion. Jack forgot the little fine and costs against him in the Probate court, and to jog his memory the sheriff levied on the saloon property. That reminded him and the matter was settled."

Marion Daily Star – Feb 17, 1887 [36]

A subsequent newspaper article suggested that in fact Jack did not leave Marion immediately, but instead spent some time working for Lizzie at the White Pigeon. Lizzie's future husband appeared for the first time in print with Lizzie in the Feb. 15, 1889, *Marion Daily Star*[37] which reported:

> "Jack Larzelere and Lizzie Lape and Dan Fritz and his wife were arrested Thursday afternoon under indictments for keeping houses of ill fame and held for trial with each under $800 bond for appearance at trial."

Jack and Lizzie, Dan and Martha – old friends in an older business. The $800 bond wasn't cheap. Marion's establishment was turning up the heat on Jack and his friends. Yet this time, flight wasn't so easy an option for Lizzie. She owned the Pigeon, and she couldn't take it with her. Or could she? Mae West had a line that pertained, "Good girls go to heaven; bad girls go everywhere."[38]

> "Police Sergeant Ed Dunn arrested John Larzelere and Lizzie Larzelere for keeping a house of assignation at the old Jack DeWitt place just north of the city. The officer took a girl named May Flowers from the place and placed her in custody of her parents who live on Bell Street. She is aged 15. Several days ago she was taken to the house by a young man who left her in charge of the keeper of the place. Both prisoners were arraigned in police court and upon pleading not guilty gave bonds to appear for trial this morning. John Larzelere pleaded guilty this morning and was fined $50 and costs while the other case was dismissed."

Akron Beacon Journal – May 31, 1890[39] *Same Story, Different Digs – Lizzie's New North Akron Locale*

She'd married, moved, opened a new franchise in less than a year, and acquired a bouncer in the form of her new husband Jack Larzelere. Lizzie the entrepreneur!

But in business and in court, things soured quickly between Jack and Lizzie because this story appeared in the *Akron Beacon Journal* on Sept. 27, 1890: [40]

> "A divorce was today granted to Lizzie Larzelere and she was restored to her maiden name of Lizzie Lape and given possession of all her property."

Most amusing to a born Lape is the fact that Lizzie took back her first husband's surname "Lape", claiming it as her maiden name, instead of Rogers. No one back home in Whitley, Kentucky could draw a straight line to our Lizzie. It was just the same when looking for 'Lizzie Rogers' among the many houses of ill repute that peppered the 1870 Chicago census. She didn't leave much of a trail in her earliest years. A purposeful deceit, if she was trying to avoid the law. It was clear that the public had developed a voracious appetite for all things Lizzie. She was becoming as popular with the reporters and editors in Akron as she was in Marion. A common case of her reputation preceding her.

CHAPTER 16

Minding the Store

I couldn't behave like other women – the house was forever uppermost in my mind.

- [Madam] Polly Adler, "A House Is Not A Home"[41]

While expanding the brand in Akron, Lizzie hired Dan Fritz and his wife Mattie to run the White Pigeon operation, over a twelve year period ending somewhere after 1901. Dan was a sturdy fellow, nine years older than Lizzie, who never backed away from a bar room brawl. He handled the saloon, while his wife Mattie occasionally ran the adjacent "house" for Lizzie. Dan would tangle with any trouble and wasn't afraid of cracking heads or gun play inside or out of the White Pigeon. There was plenty of both. Dan fought crooked bartenders, errant "doves" or "inmates" as the papers liked to refer to the women who worked there, thieving criminals, cheating husbands and angry wives, as well as the steady flow of drunks and degenerates that favored the White Pigeon with their business. Located near the rail line on the west end of town, the Pigeon had a steady clientele of transients and trouble.

However, when Officers Masterson, Monahan, Murphy and a perennial favorite Marshall Blain arrived on the scene, Dan's fists opened. Dan didn't fight the law; he pulled out his wallet. When the law stepped in, Dan paid his fair share – ten dollars here; twenty-five dollars there. Then another raid and a repeat of the monthly process. Both sides must have considered it the Original Sin tax, which it surely was. Lizzie was an astute businesswoman to have retained local son Dan Fritz as keeper of her White Pigeon. To have someone she could trust while she was away was essential to her growing the business.

The White Pigeon had it all – the lovelorn, the lust, the lushes, libelous landlords and truant tenants, plus good old comic relief. The White Pigeon was full of life, at its messiest. But, the newspapers of this era never exceeded the bounds of propriety in their reporting. Quite the opposite, they went out of their way to avoid explicit words we would hear today such as prostitute, whore, sex acts, hooker, pimp – these were taboo, too coarse for the general public's ears. A story was mostly reported between the lines, more subtly and frequently much more illustrative and humorous. Finding subtlety in an article about a bordello raid is not just ridiculous, it is downright funny.

Like it or not, the White Pigeon and similar saloons and "houses" had a prominent place in early America. Don't look for them in the history books. Try Page Two of the local papers, because there was and always will be a local audience hungry for neighborhood gossip. People in Marion knew and understood Dan Fritz, local boy, trying to make a living keeping order in a disorderly world. He was one of "their own", as were Editor Warren Harding and Marshall Blain. If there was a church on every corner of Marion, there was also a saloon and a bordello around the corner on a side street. Places like the White Pigeon, the Blue Goose, the Yellow Canary, and the White Dove all helped pay for schools, augment police officer's take-home and start Warren G. Harding toward the White House. Note the White Pigeon didn't start out white:

> "The 'red house', unless it is repainted, in no more. The painters have been at work on that famous building and it now, from without, is pure white. The purity of what now might be called the White Pigeon, does not extend further than the outer walls."

Marion Daily Star – Sept. 23, 1892 [42]

CHAPTER 17

Up to Her Pretty Neck

Lizzie and Jack's divorce announcement in the *Akron Beacon Journal* left me wondering just exactly what *"given possession of all her property"* meant. Four of her curious descendants took a field trip to the Marion County Courthouse to discover what Lizzie had possessed – beyond her personal charm.

The sandstone courthouse was built in 1884 just before Lizzie arrived in Marion. She would have climbed the same steps many times to face the court and a jury of her peers. This was Lizzie's field of battle and she was up to it.

Upon our arrival, we were directed to a walk-in vault in the Court of Common Pleas with massive black and gold stenciled doors whose un-oiled brass bolts froze open long ago.

Marion County Courthouse: Built 1884

Lizzie's court documents take up more than their fair share of this 20' x 20' historic storage room.

She wasn't just *there*; Lizzie was all over the place – in journals and indices, ledgers, dockets and in every dusty corner of this ancient space. Lizzie left a trail of debts with Marion shopkeepers and many breweries. She owed the Leisy Brewing Company; the Marion Brewing & Bottling Company; Lang, Schenk & Co.; the John Lust & Son Co.; the Marion Department Co. and H. W. Sager. A lot of people were owed a mint of money. She was sued by "renters" at the White Pigeon, and by the City of Marion during eminent domain proceedings; she was sued by the State of Ohio for "the sale of illegal liquor in a house of ill fame" and she was sued by husbands and even her own son – but put that one on the back burner. Town citizens must have erected this courthouse in anticipation of the increased work volume that Lizzie would generate.

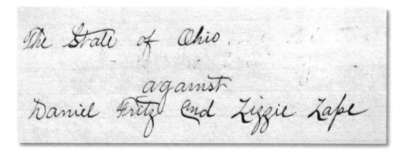

One of the dozens of legal cases involving Lizzie in the Marion County Courthouse

Our Marion researchers convened in the county Recorder's Office. If Lizzie really owned the White Pigeon, the Recorder's Office would have the proof, and it certainly did. First, the deed of purchase dated April 24, 1886, establishing that Lizzie bought the White Pigeon saloon for $1,000 from H. Gregory. Next, a deed dated December 8, 1886, conveying the adjacent "red house" to Lizzie from Sheriff Frank Beckley. Apparently, Gregory had a civil case pending in the court, so on November 27, 1886, the sheriff advertised the property for public auction and Lizzie purchased it for $995.00.

Then, an odd one. On September 13, 1890, Lizzie transferred ownership of the White Pigeon in Marion to a fellow named Lorenzo Dow Watters. A few days earlier, pursuant to a settlement in a presumed [43] child support case involving her son Arville entitled *"Lape vs. Lape et al"*; Lizzie was ordered by the court to set up a trust for him with the income and investments from the White Pigeon, which Watters was to oversee until the boy reached 25 years, at which time the White Pigeon and its assets would become his. What an inheritance! The trust was filed on Sept. 8, 1890, Jeremiah Lape's death date. Lorenzo received $1,000 from the proceeds of the arrangement.

1890 was a busy year for my family, with lawsuits in at least three Ohio counties: the Pigeon was in Marion County; Jeremiah lived in Plain City in Madison County; and the child support case in Summit County.

My southern belle of a great-great-grandma was working as a madam at the White Pigeon, for the benefit of her young son Henry Arville, until he reached age 25! Consider for a moment, the craziness of this trust. On the one hand, the court in effect endorsed her continued shady business; while on the other hand, John Law was regularly raiding the place and fining her for running a bordello. A unique application of "justice" to be sure.

"Who", you may ask, "is Lorenzo D. Watters?" Why, he was the mayor of Akron, Ohio.

Courtesy of <u>The History of Akron</u> website – www.ci.akron.oh.us [11]

CHAPTER 18

The Mayor of Akron

By all accounts, Lorenzo Dow Watters was a model mayor. He was educated in the public schools of Lancaster, Ohio, moved to Akron with his parents and family, attended Buchtel College and was admitted to the bar in 1879. He was a three-term mayor of Akron 1883-4, 1885-6, and 1893-4, and was a friend to many, encouraging defendant and plaintiff to settle out of court whenever possible. At one time, he had more court cases pending in Summit County than any other lawyer and was considered a possible contender for the state of Ohio governorship. Yet, there were far fewer articles to be found about Lorenzo than about Lizzie by a factor of one to 30.

How Lorenzo came to be involved in Lizzie's child support case is unknown. The Summit County Court of Common Pleas filing No.14800 for *Lape vs. Lape et al* has not been located. In fact, all that is known about this Summit County case is in the land recorders reference in Marion County. To sue a woman for child support was almost unheard of in late 19th century. To create a trust from the property and earnings of an illegal operation was simply bizarre.

Who was the instigator of this lawsuit? There are several possibilities. First, Lizzie may have plotted to steal Jeremiah's nest egg to buy the White Pigeon. Jeremiah Lape was dying. Certainly the court case was in progress before he died, but the final land transfers to the trust occurred on the exact day Jeremiah died. A coincidence? Son Arville was a handful by everyone's standard, and may have been a juvenile delinquent detained in a boy's school in Lancaster, Ohio. Jerry's many siblings may have decided to pursue Lizzie for child support after Jerry died. And why not soldier and law enforcer Jerry Lape et al vs. Lizzie Lape? He had plenty of motive and he most assuredly had his Plain City police officer's connections in the courts.

Another equally plausible reason for *Lape vs. Lape et al*, was that Lorenzo Dow

Watters, former two-term mayor of Akron, might have been looking for a cause célèbre to help him regain the job, which he most assuredly did after winning this case. Lizzie was busy making a muddy splash in the Akron papers earlier in 1890 with her shady house and trips to the pokey. She was a woman who owned property out of town. And she had a son who may have roamed the streets of Akron, getting into trouble by age 12. It was a new age of freedom and excess. Someone had to protect the townsfolk from themselves. That someone might have been the well-respected, civic-minded and highly-motivated Watters.

Why else would a politician publicly involve himself in the ownership and administration of a house of ill fame? His name is coupled with Lizzie's everywhere. The responsibility for the White Pigeon remaining open as long as it did rested squarely on the shoulders of the man who protected it from Lizzie's creditors. More importantly, Lorenzo's trustee connection with the Pigeon must have influenced local judges and policemen to refrain from exercising the full measure of the law against her. Lizzie had protection, and knew it.

Reformation was a new and politically-charged wind blowing through town. The newspapers were full of the stories of pauper orphan children of honored dead war heroes. County and state governments were under fire for not finding aid for these innocents. There were many reports of pathetic conditions in institutions that housed children left homeless and destitute by the Civil War. For Lorenzo, it might have been a two-edged political sword – as protector of young Arville, son of veteran soldier Jeremiah Lape, 54th OVI; and as punisher of the fallen woman Madam Lizzie.

Lorenzo Dow Watters – reformer or do-gooder? Or simply a lawyer who liked to eat. Lorenzo took up Arville's cause between his second and third term as mayor of Akron. His legal expertise cost Lizzie – and indirectly Arville – one thousand dollars ($1,000) – the original purchase price of the White Pigeon. Lorenzo must have subscribed to Mark Twain's axiom:

> *"Do good when you can, and charge when you think they will stand it."*
>
> *-Mark Twain*

CHAPTER 19

The Bigger Pond

Akron was the City on the Summit, quite literally the highest spot in Summit County, and a place of real opportunity for women like Lizzie and future generations of working women. There was a sea change coming. Women were beginning to own property and were fighting for and holding onto it in the courts. Women were getting married and divorced – a lot, making contracts and dissolving contracts which were enforced by the courts. Women were working outside of the home. Akron and other cities were growing so fast there were jobs for any and all able bodies regardless of gender. With the advent of the Industrial Revolution, women suddenly had more discretionary time. Literally hundreds of women's clubs sprang up in the bigger cities, many related to church activities, but many new ones with civic responsibilities. Women were fighting for and winning their freedom: all kinds of women, all kinds of freedom, all kinds of vice.

There were 28,000 people living in Akron in 1890 compared to just 8,300 in Marion. In the 1890-91 City Business Directory[45] for Akron, there were 65 saloons, not counting the sample and billiard rooms. There were less than 30 churches. John C. DeWitt, known as "Jack" or "J. C.", and Lizzie's future employer, was a long-time Akron resident according to the June, 1880 census. John's occupation was listed as "ship's carpenter". Listed as well were his wife, Mary, and two sons. According to the 1883-1884 city directory, John had changed professions and become a saloon keeper, as noted by this inviting advertisement:

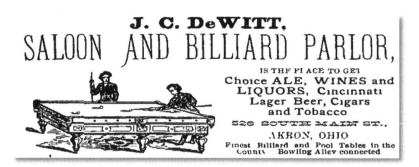

"Sample Room"? What exactly was a "sample room"? A colorful description was recorded in 1876 by a visiting Australian commission to the 1876 Philadelphia Exhibition:

> *"The drinking places are very numerous in all the large American cities, and are divided into what are termed ' saloons' and ' sample rooms.' The saloons more or less resemble the German ' bier halles' or beer halls. They are generally owned and conducted by Germans. The staple drink in them is lager-beer, which is made to produce considerable foam or head on being drawn from the keg or barrel, which is placed on a stand behind the bar counter, but which has a very small proportion (only three or four per cent.) of alcohol in it. The sample rooms are devoted principally to the sale of spirituous liquors, American ('Bourbon' and 'Rye') whisky having by far the largest sale. There is nothing but a bar in them with an extensive display of liquors, and there are no seats as in the lager-beer saloons. These 'sample rooms' are specially adapted for the form of drinking termed 'liquoring up,' or its Australian synonym 'shouting.' These establishments are principally in the hands of Irish, Scotch, or English, but by far the largest proportion, are owned by Irish."* [46]

Report of the Commissioners for Victoria Australia to His Excellency the Governor for the Philadelphia Exhibition of 1876

The line between "saloon" and "sample room" may have blurred between 1876 and 1883. Clearly, J. C. DeWitt's operation *was* more than a beer hall. Not only were liquors "choice", but entertainment was exceptional with the "Finest Billiard and Pool Tables in the County".

There were no Lape or Larzelere listings, so Lizzie was probably not living in

Akron in 1887 when this directory was compiled. By this time, J. C. DeWitt had moved from his South Main Street location to a saloon and restaurant business on the north side of Akron, near Bettes Corners. The saloon and house may well have been the "half way" house between Cuyahoga Falls and downtown Akron mentioned in the Akron Beacon Journal article on May 31, 1890, about Lizzie and Jack Larzelere's arrest, "for keeping a place of assignation at the old Jack DeWitt place just north of the city".

No railroad scout could have been more assiduous than Lizzie at locating this, her next whistle stop. With the divorce from Jack Larzelere finalized in Summit County on September 27, 1890, she promptly married the youngest son of J. C. DeWitt her employer – Harry C. DeWitt on October 27, 1890, in Canton, Stark County, Ohio. Harry was 11 years her junior, and Lizzie's fourth husband of record including – Jeremiah Lape (13 years her senior), George W. Hoffman (two years older than Lizzie), John Larzelere (same age), and now Harry C. DeWitt (11 years younger).

Lizzie and Harry were married in Canton, the location of one of the most notorious red light districts in the Midwest, also known as the "Tenderloin". A primarily woman-managed district, as were most of the houses in Lizzie's day, these brothels often operated on the second floors of many legitimate saloons, cigar and confectioner's stores and pool halls. Each brothel might employ three or four women of the night, who were more competitively concerned with how the house was decorated on the inside, than their unkempt slummy exterior appearance. Locked and bolted tighter than a drum during the day, these doors and windows opened wide after dark, as the ladies of the evening promoted their competitive advantages.[47] The streets of Canton's Tenderloin were a veritable peepshow.

Canton nightlife offered top shelf burlesque shows at the nearby State Theater, which prevailed well into mid-20th century, although the interiors of the houses grew more shabby and shopworn, not unlike the inmates. The Tenderloin was past prime. So densely-packed were bawdy houses that to deter perpetual lusty knocks at the door, it was necessary to post "Private Residence" signs on house fronts of purely residential dwellings.

Was Lizzie part of the earliest version of this Canton scene? No evidence, beyond her marriage there, has been uncovered. Still, Lizzie would have been perfectly at home in this environment, and even more likely: it would have been the logical setting for the seduction of young Mr. Harry DeWitt.

80 • LOOKING FOR LIZZIE

Ohio Saloon before 1910 [48]

Chapter 20

Happily Ever

Harry DeWitt was the youngest child of John C. and Mary DeWitt. In the Akron 1885 directory he is listed as boarding with his father. Things were starting to look up for Harry even before he met Lizzie. He was put in charge of running his father's saloon at the "half way place". And in fact, Harry and his family had moved to a residence not far from their business.

Harry and J. C. resided at the same address. Brother John's new saloon was located nearby. Becoming an independent businessman, like his brother, must have been part of Harry's big plan, or Lizzie's.

Harry was a hot head. He had the nickname "Snakes" DeWitt from the snake eyes denoting two on a pair of dice. Gambling wasn't just his business, it was his hobby. Unfortunately, he didn't have a head for the business part of his hobby. He made a wild bet on Lizzie. She on the other hand, wasn't gambling at all. Hers was a business move all the way.

On Feb. 13, 1891, the Akron Beacon Journal reported that Mrs. Harry (Lizzie) DeWitt was arrested and fined again for running a house of assignation. It was seemingly old news, but something about this arrest must have altered the atmosphere at 113 Lods Ave.

> **First Edition**
>
> **INTO THE MUD.**
>
> Saloon Keeper DeWitt Throws His Wife Out of Buggy.
>
> This morning serious complaint was made at police headquarters against Harry DeWitt, keeper of the "half way place" between Akron and Cuyahoga Falls. DeWitt had been having trouble with his wife for the last week or more. This morning Mrs. DeWitt started for Akron in a new buggy. DeWitt protested against her going and when she started from home he ran out into the street and stopped the horse, turning it about and upset the buggy. Mrs. DeWitt was thrown out into the mud. She was not hurt but the buggy was somewhat demolished. The affray was lively for a time and interesting developments are expected in court.

Akron Beacon Journal, March 19, 1891 [49]

"A lively affray" indeed! Not the kind of deference that Lizzie would have expected from young Harry. Two days later she filed for divorce.

The buggy dumping tipped the scales. Young Harry was too volatile and violent in his passion for Lizzie. Lizzie could not manage Harry and furthermore she had significant financial interests to protect. Finances first and foremost, Lizzie decided to free herself of this husband. But how?

> Lizzie Dewitt, through her attorney, L. D. Watters, sues Harry Dewitt for divorce, and equitable relief and prays that he be enjoined from disposing of property and household effects. The cause alleged is extreme cruelty. In her petition she states that she was married Oct. 27, 1890, in Canton; that she has lived with him as a faithful wife but that he has conducted himself toward her with extreme cruelty. That he, on the 27th day of February, 1891, slapped her and threw her on the floor with great force, disabling her for a term of three weeks; that on March 19, 1891, he jerked her out of a buggy and severely injured her and that on several occasions he has threatened to kill her. The petition also states that she is the possessor of certain property in Marion, O., to the value of $6,000 and that the household effects belong to her and prays that she be secured in her possession of them.
>
> Harry Dewitt and his wife have several times figured conspicuously before the people as the keepers of the "Half Way House" between Akron and Cuyahoga Falls, at a recent date having been convicted and sentenced for keeping a house of assignation at that point. An answer will probably be filed by the defendant and will probably be quite sensational.

Akron Beacon Journal- March 21, 1891 [50]

Lorenzo Dow Watters to Lizzie's rescue! …correction… to the White Pigeon's rescue! Lizzie's son Arville's trust property earnings, which Lorenzo was using to support and educate Arville, were now at risk in this new lawsuit against Lizzie. Without a backward glance, she'd flown the coop in Marion for richer pastures in Akron. She dumped the White Pigeon as she did her first three cuckold husbands. Marion did not spell freedom anymore for Lizzie; Akron did.

But now she was again embroiled in a fine mess of her own making with a hot-headed younger husband, who couldn't be managed anymore. Luckily for her, Lorenzo needed her as much as she needed him. At this point, one has to suspect that Lorenzo may have regretted the part he played in the original *"Lape vs. Lape et al"* lawsuit. However, Watters knew his duty was to Arville. And of course, a lawyer always got paid first. Lorenzo and Lizzie teamed up and threw the first legal punch at hapless Harry. She sued Harry for divorce claiming extreme cruelty. In the lawsuit she described how Harry had thrown her to the floor disabling her for three weeks. She also related how Harry had jerked her out of the buggy a month later, injuring her, and on several other occasions threatened to kill her. The lawsuit enjoined the courts from disposing of "certain property in Marion Ohio valued at $6,000 and her household effects". Lorenzo used his social reformation platform to paint a highly unfavorable view of Harry to protect a certain White Pigeon.

On April 17, 1891, Mrs. Mary DeWitt – John's wife and Harry's mother – died. It was an illness of convenience for some. One need only consider Lizzie, Mary DeWitt's 38-year old madam daughter-in-law, to understand the full measure of this woman's suffering.

Mary C. DeWitt was laid to rest at Mt. Peace Cemetery in Akron. Her marker stands tall.

Her son William H. and daughter-in-law Latisha are buried nearby. If J. C. DeWitt is buried alongside Mary, his death date is not marked on her stone. Nor are Harry and Lizzie anywhere in this snug DeWitt family plot.

"A case with a *vexing problem...* ...*What he wants to know is whether his wife Lizzie, is his mother or not*... A divorce case in which Harry desires to absolve relations with his "*better half*" is now pending in the upper courts… The affidavit declares that *father-in-law and daughter-in-law* have been intimate… Both prisoners…waived an examination…through *their* attorney, L. D. Watters."

Lizzie, Lizzie… having tracked you through several states and counties, it's still a wonder to see that all the men are willing to play the fool for you! Why even the newspaper and court reporters weren't talking about Mary DeWitt's "death by daughter-in-law". Harry was naive enough to think that things got bad *no earlier* than May 1st. Lorenzo was ever hopeful that he could get out of this mess with his political career intact, and John was conniving enough to think he could outfox this younger woman. Dreamers, all.

POLICE COURT PROCEEDINGS.

HARRY DEWITT CAUSES THE ARREST OF HIS FATHER AND WIFE ON BAD CHARGES.

A case with a vexing problem involved, came up in police court this morning. Harry DeWitt has been trying to solve the question but gave it up in despair and turned it over to Mayor Miller. What he wants to know, is whether his wife Lizzie, is his mother or not, so he declared to a group of assembled officers in the court room this morning. A divorce case in which Harry desires to absolve relations with his "better half" is now pending in the upper courts. While the state of uncertainty as to the outcome of the bill exists, Harry and Lizzie have not been living together. On April 17, 1891, Mrs. John DeWitt died, leaving John DeWitt, Harry's father a widower.

Yesterday, Harry appeared in Mayor's Court and swore out warrants for the arrest of his father, John Dewitt, on a charge of fornication, and for Lizzie DeWitt, his wife, on a charge of adultery. The affidavit declares that father-in-law and daughter-in-law have been intimate from May 1 to June 5.

Both prisoners appeared in court this morning, pleaded not guilty, waived an examination through their attorney, L. D. Watters, and was bound over to the Probate Court with bond fixed at $100 in each case.

Akron Beacon Journal – July 10, 1891 [50]

> **SHOT TO KILL.**
>
> **"JACK" DEWITT'S PLACE BURGLARIZED BY HIS OWN SON.**
>
> Beacon and Republican Correspondence.

> **SHOT TO KILL.**
>
> **"JACK" DEWITT'S PLACE BURGLARIZED BY HIS OWN SON.**
>
> Beacon and Republican Correspondence.

Akron Beacon Journal – August 25, 1891 [51]

> Harry Dewitt, better known as "Snakes" Dewitt, last night broke into the place of his father, "Jack" Dewitt. He aroused him from his slumbers and as Harry jumped from the window his father fired twice after him. Jack Dewitt this morning had a warrant sworn out for his arrest for house breaking.

If ever a woman was meant to torment man, it was Lizzie. The classic love triangle, but with a shocking warp. Poor Harry, fighting a losing battle for the love of Lizzie, a madam right down to her shiny black leather high top boots, and J. C., having recently lost his wife, either through illness or neglect, was looking for a new lease on love, and thinking he could do better than his son Harry. All he needed to do was to treat her right – as he did his first wife of 34 years. In the meantime, the Akron papers were making a mint of money on the 'perils of being Lizzie'. But unlike the beautiful Pauline tied to the tracks, our Lizzie was full speed ahead.

CHAPTER 21

After

On October 14, 1891 Lizzie got her divorce from Harry, one week short of a full year of connubial "bliss". The newspaper gave it short shrift, announcing only that a divorce was granted without alimony.

Lizzie was free again, but not for long. Three weeks later, it was recorded in the Akron, Summit County Marriage Book[52] that Lizzie Rogers had married John C. DeWitt. It was official, Lizzie chose father over son – a new partner 18 years older than she, instead of 11 years younger.

*Miss Rogers marries Mr. DeWitt, giving truth to the quote,
"I am my own ex-daughter-in-law."*

Why did Lizzie marry for a fifth time? She had been through a lot in the courts to recover the property that she brought to each marriage. Why risk it again? In 1853, the year that Lizzie Rogers was born, Susan B. Anthony campaigned for the expansion of married women's rights to property ownership. Prior generations of women ceded their property rights to their husbands when they married. Lizzie's generation was the first to feel the full freedom of property ownership protection by the courts. Fear of destitution no longer motivated Lizzie or thousands of other unhappily married women to *stay* in bad marriages. They could take their fair share of the money and depart. And they did – in droves. The divorce rate skyrocketed.

Maybe it was love that motivated Lizzie to marry Harry's father J. C.? More likely Lizzie was scheming for something more tangible – a solid husband less likely to run around, a business partner of equal ambition, a less volatile version of young Harry, a man of means – a "Sugar Daddy" to a 38-year old woman who never had a childhood. But things hadn't cooled off as much as the divorce court reporter imagined.

J. C. DeWitt's home might be the white frame house visible behind the billboard at extreme right [53]

> Nov 10, 1891
>
> ## TOOTH AND NAIL.
>
> ### HARRY DEWITT SAILS INTO HIS FATHER, JOHN.
>
> Harry Dewitt and his father John are in trouble again and have been arrested charged with disorderly conduct. Since John stole his son's wife, Harry has led a dissolute life. He is without money or occupation and his sole object seems to be to get even with his father. This morning Harry met his father and his divorced wife on North Howard street in front of Boder's meat market. The instant he saw John he sailed into him, hitting him twice in the face. For a few minutes the father and son had a lively scrimmage and tongue lashing contest on the sidewalk. Harry soon ran out into the street and called for an officer to come and arrest him. Officers Harris and Guillet responded and gave the case their attention. Harry claims that his father married his divorced wife yesterday.

Akron Beacon Journal – November 10, 1891 [54]

The trouble with Harry was perhaps best revealed in the line – "Harry soon ran out into the street and called for an officer ***to come and arrest him.***" Harry was asking the officer to arrest himself? This can only mean that Harry was afraid of what he might do to his father J. C. and recognized that he was out of control, due to a drinking problem. Not that the papers mentioned this. But then again, "depressing" doesn't sell papers like "lively" or "sensational."

Poor Harry! Cooler heads prevailed to bring about a resolution to this vexing problem. J. C. wanted reconciliation, and Harry just plain ran out of money. J. C. settled the payment of Harry's bond, and Harry agreed to dismiss charges, since there were none that would stick. J. C. was exhibiting some of those traits that Lizzie found so attractive. It was a touching family reconciliation, and as usual the newspaper was there to write the end to this serial saga in Lizzie's life.

> **PEACE NOW REIGNS.**
>
> **THE DEWITTS, FATHER AND SON, HAVE SETTLED MATTERS SATISFACTORILY.**
>
> "Jack" Dewitt's case did not come to trial before 'Squire Anderson to-day. The attorneys in the case with "Jack" and his son Harry held a star chamber session in an ante-room of the 'Squire's court and there agreed to quash the matter. The particulars of settlement were that Harry should dismiss the charges of assault and battery in 'Squire Anderson's court, on condition that his father sign his bond in Mayor Miller's court.
>
> "Jack" then opened his soul toward his son and agreed not to appear against him in Probate Court, if Harry would not interfere with him and his wife. Peace now reigns between father and son. 'Squire Anderson feels slighted that no provision was made for the payment of a bill of $8.10, costs made in the case.

Akron Beacon Journal – November 11, 1891 [55]

Except somebody forgot to pay the judge, Squire Anderson.

Lizzie's Tree - grows

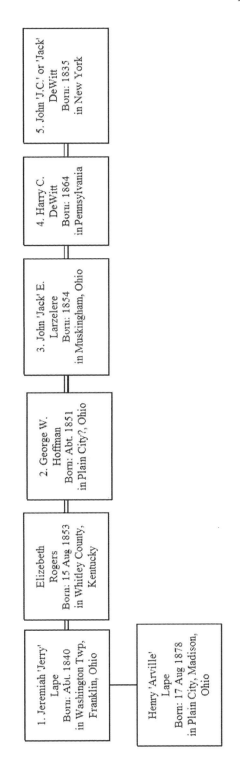

CHAPTER 22

Guarding Arville

With all of Lizzie's travails, few noticed that a little 12-year old boy named Henry Arville Lape was growing up among the barbarians. Arville may not have thought of them as uncivilized, since they were all the family he'd known since the last step-father was given the boot. Still, Lorenzo D. Watters was having an impact, and it may have saved our whole family.

On April 29, 1891, J. C. DeWitt had made application for guardianship of "Henry O. Lape", stating that he, J. C., was the brother of Henry's father – Jeremiah **DeWitt**, which was a bunch of hogwash. Henry Arville Lape was not his nephew, just his future stepson. Still, one has to hand it to J. C. to step forward and generously offer to take an orphan under his wing just 12 days after his wife Mary died. It was just the sort of thing Lizzie would have wished for in a father-in-law… oops, future fiancé.

Apparently one good turn wasn't all that he had in mind, so J. C. went ahead and applied for Jeremiah Lape's military pension accruing to Arville. Over the course of the next four and a half years J. C. DeWitt continued to draw this pension as Arville's guardian. Raising Arville would help support several families in Akron and Marion – the Fritz, DeWitt and Watters families most directly. In 1891, Arville appeared for the first time in the Akron city directory, seemingly living on his own at 313 North Howard. Odd, because he was just 13 years old. But where were his mother Lizzie and stepfather J. C.?

Lizzie, J. C., and Harry DeWitt appear nowhere in this 1891-1892 directory. A *Mrs. L. Marquard* was operating their saloon at the previous North Howard address. Did Lizzie and Jack C. DeWitt abandon 13-year old son Arville in Akron? Was Lorenzo D. Watters shepherding Arville from his lawyerly perch? Possibly. Lorenzo wasn't re-elected as mayor until 1893. More likely, the J. C. DeWitt family was simply in the middle of a move or laying low, using Arville's name as a beard for their continued presence in the city. By this time, J. C.'s brother William DeWitt was now listed in nearby Cuyahoga Falls operating a dining hall. Perhaps Lizzie and J. C. were lending a hand. Plus, there was a new DeWitt saloon in town listed as "Sample room, imported and domestic wines, liquors and cigars" at 728 South Main, with residence. However, this saloon was listed under *Solomon*, not John, DeWitt. This was a block or two away from John's original bar at 526 South Main.

A DeWitt syndicate seemed to be emerging, stretching from South Akron into Cuyahoga Falls. Lizzie seemed to have gotten herself some *famiglia* connections by marrying John C. DeWitt. It was a consortium – purveyors of whiskey, women, tobacco, entertainment and gambling – with blood connections. That Lizzie would be involved was entirely logical because of her profession. Prostitution had been a part of organized crime for centuries before and after Lizzie. There was a steady flow of legal transactions that surrounded Lizzie's activities in Marion and then in Summit County and she was able to use top legal advisors to protect herself in a way unheard of before or even during her era. In Akron, the DeWitts bought, sold and rented properties, and there were a few odd one dollar land transfers between non-family members. One suspect purchase of land from a Probate Judge suggested there might have been some "horse trading" due to gambling debts or for other nefarious reasons.

Arville's Guardianship[56] payout to J. C. DeWitt – who claimed falsely that he was Arville's uncle.

Chapter 23

Mr. Dow and Mr. Winn

On November 8, 1892, the City of Akron's leadership changed hands. Out with the "ins" – an exclusive group of Republicans with an iron grip on City Hall. Until that date, Akron had been a Republican bastion made up of business leaders. In the 1890's, the population of Akron was straining at its seams, and there were widespread outbreaks of smallpox and cholera. Public drunkenness, excessive gambling and debauchery were causing the city's leaders to take steps to keep the city safe for men, women, children, and new business. Nothing turned off a new partner in an Akron investment like disreputable city conditions, and the Republicans were forced to make some changes for the well-being of all. The Republicans were out and the Democrats were in, but not before certain new protectionist taxes were enacted, or extracted as the case may be.[57]

The politics of regulating the use and abuse of alcohol had long been debated in America. Akron and other big cities in Ohio such as Columbus, Cleveland and Cincinnati were heavily settled by German-Americans whose breweries' biggest customer was the corner saloon[58]. In Lizzie's Akron, saloons and houses of ill-repute went together like burgers and fries. The face of morality in America was slipping. Churches and women's groups called on their politicians for a change. Ohio was at the apex of the early temperance movement with women and children marching and protesting in front of neighborhood saloons in small towns such as Hillsboro, Ohio in 1873. The negative PR hurt the German braumeisters' lucrative business, and in turn regulations limiting the protesting arose in the very same cities where beer was brewed, Columbus, Cincinnati and Cleveland[59]. In 1886, Republican Ohio Governor James Foraker enacted the Dow Law, named for Civil War veteran General Neal S. Dow, considered to be one of the great early leaders of the temperance movement. The new law went into effect just in time for the grand opening of Lizzie's White Pigeon in Marion.

The Dow "sin tax" hit Lizzie's business hard. She immediately had to start paying $200 per saloon per year. This tax rose annually and steadily during the time Lizzie was in business until by 1906, she was taxed $1,000 annually for each of her saloons. That was a lot of money, considering that the White Pigeon was purchased for a total of $1,995. Did the Dow tax cause Lizzie to look for revenues elsewhere, beyond the bar room door?

The legislators must have concluded that one taxed sin deserved another, because by May of 1894, the Winn Law was enacted, stating it was unlawful to sell liquor in a house of ill fame. This legislation was named for John W. Winn, attorney and Anti-Saloon League representative from Defiance, Ohio. Once enacted, the bill created a perfect storm of judicial activity. At its most absurd, within the language of the law, there was a finder's fee for discoverers of Winn sin trafficking. Any random fellow on the street, including the fully-served customer, could sue a saloon/house for a percentage of the successfully collected tax. What was an honest madam to do? On one hand, Lizzie had to pay the Dow Tax if she was selling liquor in her saloon or in her house. On the other, it was illegal to sell it in her house or the courts had the right to attach her property for collection of the Winn Tax. What a perplexing situation for owners of a full-service operation such as Lizzie's! Not to worry, in 1896 Ohio Attorney General Monuett attempted to clarify this troublesome point:

> "A doubt arose in the mind of the assessor whether the Winn law, prohibiting the sale or giving away of intoxicants in houses of ill fame, would not make it illegal to receive the Dow tax from a saloon connected with such a house. Attorney-general Monuett took the position that the assessor had no right to presume that the keeper of a saloon intended to run his establishment in an unlawful way. The collection of the tax does not authorize the saloonkeeper to violate the Winn law any more than any other law regulating the sale of liquor. The opinion concludes as follows:
>
> "Therefore in my opinion they should be listed as sellers of intoxicating liquors in a lawful way. Each separate and unlawful act

of selling or giving away intoxicating liquors, either in a house of ill fame or any other unlawful purpose constitutes an offense punishable by law. An assessor cannot determine this in advance and should not list them as keepers of houses of ill fame, but as sellers of intoxicating liquors." [60]

Ohio Legal News, Volume 3, Jay Ford Laning, 1896

Mr. Dow and Mr. Winn were determined to tax Lizzie's operations to the full extent of the law. They had her over a barrel.

Akron City Directory (Burch) Advertisement [61]

CHAPTER 24

What's the Big Idea?

A bed of roses was not Lizzie's lot in life, unless you include the thorns. Perhaps more than any other husband, John C. DeWitt was Lizzie's match in ambition and raw determination. They had plans for an empire of adult entertainment in Akron, Ohio, long before Las Vegas was surveyed. This couple should have been perfect partners in petty crime and likely they were for a time. A brewery would have been delighted to service their accounts and be in their good graces during the height of their reign over keg and couch. But the DeWitt duo went from dynamic to dynamite in less time than it takes for beer to go flat.

The fuse was lit when someone got greedy, or should we say greedier than the other. Lizzie fired the first shot. She usually did. The *Akron Beacon Journal index* for 1894 summed it up nicely:

> June 1: Elizabeth DeWitt files petition for appointment of receiver in partnership dissolution suit against John C. DeWitt.
>
> June 14: Case dismissed.
>
> July 17: John C. DeWitt sues for divorce by Elizabeth.
>
> July 23: Restraining order continued.

She did what she had always done when threatened with marital property loss: Lizzie hired a good lawyer. This time, they both had more to lose. Through the years, J. C. DeWitt had owned or rented many properties in and around Akron.

Even more improbably, J. C. DeWitt owned a steamer called the New Republic berthed at Lakeside Park on Summit Lake, not far from Lizzie's recently purchased new property at 169 Bartges Street.

Or maybe not so improbable after reading an excerpt from *The Social Evil in Chicago, by the Vice Commission, 1911:*

> "During the summer the excursion boats are often floating assignation houses... The state rooms are rented many times in the course of three or four hours... The law regarding the use of boats for prostitution purposes should be enforced... The owners of lake steamers should exercise more vigilance enforcing their rules." [62]

The City Liquor Store at 184 South Howard would have been Lizzie's pride and joy. J. C. and she certainly planned a long partnership when they acquired the business. But things rapidly became rocky in her second DeWitt marriage.

The City Liquor Store was on right side (west) about four store fronts from the Schumacher Mill at end of street

ABJ JUL 17, 1894

Two Divorce Suits Commenced—The Recorders Annual Report—An Answer and Cross Petition—Probate Items and Court News.

Elizabeth DeWitt seeks a divorce from her husband, John C. DeWitt. The petition states that they were married November 7, 1891. That since marriage the plaintiff has always been a faithful, loving and obedient wife. That defendant has been guilty of extreme cruelty toward her, in that he used insulting and profane language. That the defendant has failed to furnish clothing for her. That at the time of her marriage to defendant, the plaintiff was the owner of considerable property valued at $7,000, that on June 15, 1894, the defendant went to two parties offering each $100 to swear in court that they had seen the plaintiff in rooms with men, so that he could obtain a divorce and alimony. That on December 23, 1893, the defendant induced the plaintiff to enter into partnership with him, in the wholesale liquor business at 184 South Howard street. That since this was formed he has failed to report any of the business proceedings to her. She asks for injunction, to restrain defendant from disposing of any of the property until the cause is heard. She asks for a divorce, alimony and for adjustment of all property rights between herself and defendant.

Akron Beacon Journal – July 17, 1894 [63]

"Elizabeth" (no kidding – *Elizabeth*?) fired the first volley, claiming faithful devotion on her part, extreme cruelty on his. She further alleged that he failed to provide clothing for her, and forced her into a partnership to sell liquor (a nod to the woman-as-an-extension-of-husband rule of law at the time.) She also attempted to quash his anticipated infidelity suit. What were the odds of winning a suit for faithlessness against a well-known madam?

1894 was a brutal year for Lizzie, especially in its second half. Lizzie had been living in the rear flat at 618 North Howard along with her husband J. C. and his brother and sister-in-law. At some point during the divorce proceedings she moved to 206 North Howard. That is where her son was listed in the previous year's directory.

On November 26, 1894, three days before Thanksgiving, Lizzie was badly burned when a gasoline stove exploded, presumably at her home. She and another woman named Miss Carry Hawks suffered severe but, fortunately, not life-threatening burns on the hands and face. Burns on the hands and face were disfiguring, certainly. It could not have been an easy recovery for Lizzie or her friend.

It was during this period that one of Lizzie's five children may have been born. On January 18, 1895, a baby girl was born in Columbus, Ohio, and christened in Pickaway County, not far from Plain City. She was named Edna Lape. Lizzie Lape was listed as the mother; the baby's father was not named. Edna did not appear in any other records beyond this tiny birth announcement in the county records. If Lizzie were pregnant, it would have been explosive news for the outcome of her divorce-in-progress, particularly so, if J. C. DeWitt were not the father. Leaving Akron to keep the secret birth from J. C. DeWitt would explain why the baby was born out of town, but the truth of this matter died with Lizzie and a baby named Edna.

In April of 1895, Lizzie obtained her divorce from J. C. DeWitt.

> **Divorce Case Decided.**
> Judge Voris yesterday rendered his decision in the case of Elizabeth Dewitt vs. John C. Dewitt, giving the plaintiff a divorce, custody of child, alimony and rights of property.

Judge [Di]Voris presided at three of Lizzie's divorces.
Akron Beacon Journal, April 13, 1895 [64]

What could a 42-year old madam, with five failed marriages and a 17-year old son with an odd trust fund, do exactly? Go back to work.

No more lounging on the deck of the steamer "New Republic" for Lizzie. No more plans for early retirement in the bosom of the DeWitt family. If nothing else, she was a hard working gal from Kentucky with a little alimony and a big plan.

Before he was cut out of the plan, J. C. DeWitt and Lizzie must have dreamed of something much bigger than the City Liquor partnership. That something probably included Lakeside Park at Summit Lake, a bucolic natural lake and early amusement park, well-situated for Akron traffic via a new train line.

Lakeside Park – Akron Ohio

> **CITY LIQUOR STORE.**
> **J. C. DEWITT,**
> Successor to R. L. McAllister,
> DEALER IN
> **FOREIGN and DOMESTIC WINES and LIQUORS,**
> OVERHOLT'S RYE WHISKEY A SPECIALTY
> TRY MY $200 RYE WHISKEY   184 S HOWARD STREET

1894 Akron City Business Directory[65]

Their business strategy would have included bringing their various fields of expertise – boating, liquor sales, gambling and prostitution to a venture at or near Lakeside Park. Lizzie's new house was located within two miles of Lakeside Park and the City Liquor store itself at the south end of Akron. When John DeWitt and Lizzie divorced, his half of the dream may have died, but Lizzie's did not. She simply kept moving, like a train on a downhill track.

With the divorce, she cut her ties with one of the more notorious saloon keepers in Akron and also from his extended vice-laden family franchise, losing half of their Akron enterprise through the dissolution of the business partnership. She was probably now on many breweries do-not-extend-credit lists. DeWitt's family connections ran deep in Akron, and many doors wide open before 1895 must have slammed shut. She had to move in with her son since she had lost her home with her husband's family. And she would still have been recovering from the burns she sustained in the stove explosion, which were undoubtedly a drain on her finances as well as her psyche.

If J. C. wasn't the reliable business partner she'd had in mind, then there were plenty of other candidates – one of whom entered Lizzie's life – as most others did – the very same year of her divorce – Charles W. Veon of Akron, Ohio.

CHAPTER 25

North Hill Neighbors

Charles W. Veon would have known of Lizzie when she worked north of Akron at the halfway place in Bettes Corners, first as Lizzie Larzelere, then as Mrs. Harry DeWitt, followed by Mrs. John C. DeWitt. Charles' family had lived for years in that small corner of North Akron. And, Lizzie would have been hard to miss with the wild scenes unfolding along North Howard hill. Between the buggy dumping, shootout between father and son DeWitt, and the family fisticuffs at Boder's Market, fully covered in the *Beacon Journal*, the DeWitt family would have been the talk of the neighborhood. Charles Veon lived there with his wife Ella and their three children, as did his parents. Charles worked many jobs, sometimes for the Cleveland, Akron and Cincinnati Railway Company, with his older brother and his father.

On January 8, 1895, Mrs. Charles Veon – Ella – died following childbirth. Her 14 day-old baby daughter also died. Charles Veon became a widower with three children. Five years earlier in September of 1890, the *Akron Beacon Journal* reported Charles's arrest and fine for intoxication, apparently not an isolated incident. After his wife died, his children went to live with Charles' parents. Charles moved into a boarding house at 206 North Howard – the boarding house of Lizzie DeWitt.

On July 14, 1895, Lizzie and Charles W. Veon were married at St. John's Episcopal Church in Cuyahoga Falls six months after Charles' wife's death and just three months after Lizzie was divorced from J. C. DeWitt. It was a year of transition for both of them. For the first time in her life, Lizzie was married in a church, not by a justice of the peace. It was perhaps a bigger commitment than she had previously made in her other marriages. She hoped she had the right man this time – a trustworthy partner and husband. Maybe he didn't have the business know-how that she brought to the partnership, but if he were an honorable husband and he trusted her business sense, then they could put her plan into action. No more derailments for Lizzie. She was on her way again.

North Howard Street & North Hill, Akron Ohio 1902 – Scene of many Lizzie Scenes[66]

CHAPTER 26

Kentucky-Grown Madams

Charles and Lizzie began their life together in the saloon previously run with J. C. DeWitt – at the City Liquor Store locale in Akron. The Veons evidently expanded Lizzie's business to include a restaurant – downright respectable. The old Jack DeWitt place boasted a sample room and restaurant, and perhaps that is where Lizzie developed an interest in cuisine. On the other hand, we could be talking pickled pigs feet and beer nuts here.

Under Akron's "Classified Business Directory" section for "Restaurants", there were 10 listed, of which Lizzie's was not one. Instead, the new "C. W. Veon" establishment appeared under "Saloons" – one of 129. With so many competitors, it must have been hard for Lizzie to differentiate herself from every Charles, Jack or Harry. But she had made a clean sweep of Jack DeWitt – he and his son Harry had cleared out of Akron. Lizzie had taken that ground.

Lizzie clearly was a person of some charm beyond her obvious career attributes. At age 43, she was well past the first blush when she married Charles. She had held the generally favorable attention of mayors and editors, politicians and policemen, lawyers, judges and jurors, and a few good men, as well. She must also have gained the respect of some of the fairer sex – or as a madam, she would have failed to marshal the ladies of the "house". She was a leader, not a follower. By her own standards, she was winning in a man's world. Today, we peer backward through a looking glass at Lizzie, thinking she allowed herself to be used by men for their own gain. But in fact, Lizzie used every means to shape a hard scrabble life into something more adventurous and creative. She was in control of her own destiny. She was not to be taken lightly, a funny thing to say about a madam.

Life was astonishingly brutal for women in the last century. It was not simply a man's world; it was a world where it was safer to be a man. Women died so frequently from childbirth and abortion complications that it was not uncommon for men to have three and four wives in one lifetime. Rape, physical abuse and other lesser forms of discrimination were crimes that went unpunished and unreported, within the confines of the immediate family. America was a wild frontier and its towns and cities were deeply troubled by lawlessness. Only limited law enforcement existed in many cities and towns on these edges of civilization.

The more subtle forms of sexual discrimination affected **all** social tiers, not just Lizzie's. Early death in childbirth or as a result of a botched abortion were great levelers. Married women typically gave up their property rights when they married. They had no political rights or legal protection from abusive husbands and parents. They could not vote. They were not allowed to teach school or work after deciding to marry. They had to quit school to help take care of younger siblings. Women had one choice – comply or live outside the social system. A "marginalized" life? Perhaps.

One such person who lived Lizzie's life was a woman named Belle Brezing of Lexington, Kentucky. Belle was a madam of high order. The American equivalent of a European courtesan, Belle started out like Lizzie in Kentucky. But more is known about Belle's life.[67] She was the illegitimate daughter of a prostitute. At age 12, the age of consent in Kentucky in 1872, she was seduced by a 36-year-old man. Their relationship lasted two years. Other relationships ensued. More illicit dealings transpired, including a mysterious accidental gunshot-to-the-head death of a paramour. Belle slid into prostitution and had a baby daughter born handicapped and raised for her by a neighbor. That might have been the end of Belle's story, except for the fact that she managed to save enough money to open her own house, then a second, followed by a third house that she enlarged to three floors and elaborately redecorated in 1895.

Madam Belle grew to become a well-known and respected businessperson in Lexington, and Governor Blackburn himself pardoned her in 1882 when she was charged with keeping a "bawdy house". She was and still is an iconic figure in Lexington, Kentucky. Belle Brezing is perhaps best known for the character drawn from her life story, in the book *"Gone With The Wind"*... Margaret Mitchell's own Belle Watling.

Sharing Belle's Kentucky roots, Lizzie was likely to have known of and admired Belle's success. Whether they knew each other personally is one of those unanswered questions. But it was a small world on the shady side of the street. Anyone working in a specialized field knows how small.

Why were there so many Lizzies and Belles in the second half of the 19th century? The War Between the States was a key factor. Many young impoverished women came out of the south, migrating to northern cities where conditions were thought to be better. Families in the south were destitute, and with their farmlands destroyed and taxes growing, the situation became impossible for many families to stay together. The most famous sister/madam team in U.S. history, the Everleigh sisters of the Chicago Levee, who claimed they were from Louisville, Kentucky (Kentucky origins again!), left their poverty-burdened family to start a new life in Chicago's red light district. It is even suggested in some accounts that the sisters' family helped them finance their early ambitions. They had a "big plan", too, and it paid off handsomely for these sisters. Having built the most opulently appointed and exclusive house of prostitution in America, the two southerners built a northern empire, and counted among their clientele, Prince Henry of Prussia – brother to the German Kaiser, Marshall Field Jr., Theodore Dreiser, Ring Lardner and heavyweight champion Jack Johnson. After 11 years of successfully operating the club with all of its prerequisite run-ins and negotiations with Chicago crime bosses, the law, and the courts – Minna and Ada Everleigh retired to New York City. These two may have led "marginal" lives, but they cut an impressive swath in clearing the way for powerful women in business.[68]

One other factor driving young women northward was an obvious one: estrogen. There had been a tragic loss of healthy eligible young men in the South. The war had decimated that segment of the population, and the less populous South was hit harder than the North. After the war, when southern women made the decision to move on with their lives, the conventional paths were blocked. To suggest that the Civil War emancipated southern women, as well as slaves, is not such a stretch when you consider that many women walked out of the south battle-weary, to become independent survivors.

Belle Brezing of Lexington, Kentucky 1859 – 1940 [69]

CHAPTER 27

Parkhursters Are Us

Lizzie and Charles Veons' honeymoon was no honeymoon. Married in July, 1895, they shared just two days of wedded bliss in Akron before Lizzie was once again plunged into litigation, this time at her White Pigeon property in Marion. As usual, it was front man Dan Fritz, not Lizzie who was initially named as the assumed property owner of the Pigeon.

> **WANT IT OPENED**
>
> "A Number of Citizens of West Marion Want West Center Street Extended."

Marion Daily Star – July 16, 1895 [70]

The City of Marion and a group of citizens wanted to extend Center Street for access by residents living near the Malleable Iron Works by acquiring property through eminent domain. The property owners of the lots affected were identified as Hoyle, Thompson, and – erroneously – Dan Fritz.

On Nov. 12, the city's condemnation case made the papers again, this time with the corrected names of the property owners including Lizzie Lape DeWitt Veon and C. W. Veon. Then, on Dec. 6, Lizzie's answer was filed in the court of common pleas. Finally, on Dec. 10, the *Marion Daily Star* reported the verdict:

> *The jury came in Monday evening... in the case of the City of Marion against Thomas Thompson and others [including Lizzie].*
>
> *The verdict allowed to T. A. Thompson and Isabella Thompson for land taken $275, to Lizzie Lape DeWitt Veon and C. W. Veon for land taken $350 and $150 damages and to Horatio Hoyles $800 for land taken and $250 damages.*

Akron lawyers, Grant & Sieber, succeeded once again in securing compensation for Lizzie[71]

There is now an alley that squeaks past the edge of where the White Pigeon saloon existed. This must have been the right of way secured by the city. There is virtually no clearance between alley and the Pigeon's foundation.

There was a threatening undercurrent to this lawsuit. It was clear the City of Marion and its good citizens were not averse to disrupting the red light district well established in the West End. Nothing like a new thoroughfare, to disrupt and remove blight. Two birds with one stone, politically speaking. Yet this lawsuit was nothing compared to other litigation that hit Lizzie concurrently. Reform was in the air. The Parkhursters were getting organized!

Dr. Charles H. Parkhurst was a New York City clergyman whose 1892 sermon electrified the nation with its condemnation of the evils of prostitution, saloon trade, and gambling in his city, compounded and unabated by a corrupt police force and political machine of Tammany Hall.

After his initial sermon, many in New York set out to dissuade him of his poor opinion. But he went undercover with several unsavory "artful dodgers" into the murky underworld of moral turpitude and original sin. Dr. Parkhurst walked the walk and documented his trail. He took witnesses and a camera with him, then returned to the pulpit and preached with an informed moral authority. In so doing, he galvanized his city as few reformers have done, before or since. With Parkhurst pointing the mirror, and Police Commissioner Teddy Roosevelt leading the charge on Tammany Hall, there was, for a time, true reform.[72] Leadership for a reform movement long overdue, swept across America, right up to and including little Marion, Ohio.

On August 6, 1895, the *Marion Daily Star*[73] headline read:

> **THE PARKHURSTERS**
>
> They Organize a Good Citizenship League Monday Evening.
> *"A campaign against the vices of the city to be commenced at once. All offenders to be looked after and punished."*

It was the opening volley by a group of church committees from Marion, strongly influenced by Dr. Parkhurst's popular book published in 1895 titled *"Municipal Reform Movements in the United States"*[74], which called individual citizens to public action. The article went on to describe their resolutions:

1. Enforce the Sunday [Blue] laws.
2. Enforce by whom, how and when liquor was sold.
3. Enforce the gambling laws.
4. "Pull" the houses of ill repute.

In regard to Lizzie's oldest profession, the *Daily Star* reporter wrote:

> *"They [the Parkhursters] are going after the houses of ill repute. They will not go slumming to find out where they are and how bad they are but will simply get after them and have each of them arrested. In other words they will have these houses pulled if the city is not ridden of them by the time they get their machinery in working order."*

Parkhurst's book and the reform movement itself were interesting studies in motivation. Citizens recognized that public servants such as the police and court systems were not able to get the job done on their own. In fact, there was little motivation on their part to shut these operations down because they were a source of revenue to each (including the lawyers). The citizen's distain for the effectiveness of the political system is apparent in the *Marion Daily Star* article. However well-intended though, the reform movement was only a skip-stone away from vigilantism. If the law wouldn't take the right measures, then they, the unelected citizens, would. Lizzie could not have rested easy in Akron after this article was published in Marion.

Interestingly, Warren G. Harding was known to have been determined to *not* take sides in this reform movement in Marion, despite efforts of friends and neighbors to gain his support. Also noted, Simon Eugene DeWolfe, chairman and head of the Good Citizenship League, was the father of Pete DeWolfe, Florence Harding's first husband, by then deceased and "killed by the drink". Simon DeWolfe had been a neighbor of Amos Kling, Florence's father. In 1895, Amos was raising Marshall DeWolfe, also Simon's grandson. There were deep undercurrents in Warren G. Harding's and Lizzie's little town of Marion, Ohio. Long standing regrets and resentments contributed to blame and retribution. Lizzie and her likes were considered enablers toward the path of self-destruction of our most precious resource, our innocent children. It was hard not to revile her choice of livelihood. But Warren Harding didn't. He had no interest in taking sides... maybe because he was privately on her side, or perhaps because she knew too much about his youthful transgressions.

CHAPTER 28

Reformer Regrets

The Parkhursters' call to arms lit a fire under several Marion public servants who were worried about mob rule. The Marion police force felt threatened by the Parkhursters' criticism and unsolicited scrutiny and was not happy to have any help on what they considered their turf. Pressure for arrests mounted, and Lizzie's lawsuit was the "first drawn" in Marion County:

> **UNDER THE NEW [WINN] LAW**
>
> Sleuth M'eldowney Goes After An Alleged Bawdy House
>
> ***"He Becomes the Plaintiff in a Suit Brought Against Daniel Fritz and Others – There's a Big Rake-off in This for the Petitioner."***
>
> The State of Ohio by James McEldowney, plaintiff, against Daniel Fritz, Lizzie Larzelere and Lorenzo Dow Watters is the title of the petition...[for Dan was selling liquor in her house]... The petition is the first drawn in this county under the act passed May 18, 1894 [Winn Law]... The section of the act which appeals most strongly to McEldowney... is probably section 8, which prescribes that one-third of the amount of the recovery... be retained by the person causing such action...
>
> *Marion Daily Star – September 7, 1895* [75]

The Winn Law had effectively pinned a WANTED poster on the White

Pigeon and promised a third of the reward bounty to the successful hunter. "Detective" James McEldowney was not a Parkhurster. But he was in town hoping to make a mint of money, if not many friends.

The Marion Parkhursters likely hired Jim McEldowney to scope out the neighborhood. He talked reform when he came to town, then lingered around Marion for weeks prior to filing the White Pigeon complaint, watching saloonists on Sundays, spying on the town pharmacist, looking for dirty deals, following up bawdy house leads. A letter to the editor of the *Marion Daily Star* exemplified the reformist movement. The "absolutely worthless police force" echoed Dr. Parkhurst's bad *boss* philosophy, suggesting citizens may need to take charge when authorities were unwilling to act:

> **COMMEND THE DETECTIVE**
>
> Editor Star: I read with interest that there has been a detective named McEldowney, in or midst gathering evidence against law-breaking saloons. The law-abiding people ought to uphold and sustain him. The slurs cast upon him by the trapped saloonists and their friends are not surprising, but the better element of Marion can offset that by commending and sustaining him. With an absolutely worthless police force, Marion stands in great need of a detective to bring lawless saloonists to order. Good for McEldowney. If the saloonist wants to combine, let them: then let law-abiding people of Marion combine once and well shall see whether law or lawlessness shall rule. – Law and Order

Marion Daily Star – September 7, 1895 [76]

But this was early in McEldowney's Marion tenure. He soon became a very unpopular man around Marion. He got himself into bondsman and girlfriend problems several times during his short stay in Marion, and was not considered a friend of the courts, the police force, and certainly not saloonists. In point of fact, he was essentially a shill for the reformists. But nobody liked a rat fink and everyone resented his finger-pointing, more so when it was wagged in the faces of honest business people in town. There were a few other filings against saloonists, but none as dramatic as the case he filed against the White Pigeon, its owners and operators.

The Marion Daily Star, October 12, 1895 edition reported:

> "In the case of the State of Ohio against Daniel Fritz and others, ... Elizabeth Veon... answers that she is the owner of the real estate...the White Pigeon, and as she has no knowledge of the truth or falsity of the facts stated in the petition, denies each and every allegation."

In the same edition of the *Star* was this exposé of McEldowney:

JIM WAS MISTAKEN

Or James Made A Mistake, Which?
Detective McEldowney Invites a Young Woman to His Boarding House, but the Mistress of the House Invites Her To Leave – 'Mac' Explains.

What Mac managed to do in Marion with his tawdry gumshoe skulking, was unify the policemen, newspapermen, *and* saloonists against him. If Mac was a hired gun of the reformists, he probably received his walking papers shortly after this article exposed his boarding house fling. Before the next year was out, he and his wife Lulu returned to Upper Sandusky. Mac must have needed reforming too, because the wife left him soon after. The Parkhursters decided that the McEldowney cure was worse than the White Pigeon condition, because he left town with his tail between his legs.

On May 20, 1896, the court in the Winn Law first Marion County test case of the *State of Ohio versus Lizzie Lape* for the sale of liquor in a house of ill-repute was *"Dismissed at costs of complainant"*. Lizzie fought and won her case by answering the court that as owner (not operator) she denied all knowledge. Not that it was as simple as that... she hired excellent lawyers and had more than a few friends in the courts and on the police force in Marion, Ohio. The new law had the unintended consequence of making it desirable for enterprising owners to hire out their property for illegal purposes. The intent of the law had been circumvented.

After the hubbub died down, things returned to normal at the White Pigeon – with routine police raids and arrests, fisticuffs, inmate squabbles, and general carousing, with payoffs as usual. The reformation had been, well, reformed.

CHAPTER 29

Studying for the Bar

Lizzie and Charles' first year together was over. 1895 had been one long round of litigation. Lizzie's divorce from Jack DeWitt; the eminent domain suit in Marion, and the Winn case at the White Pigeon had consumed money, time, and delayed Lizzie's plans. Public sentiment was fickle and Lizzie had been around long enough to know that it might be the Parkhursters and the Anti-Saloon League this season, but next season things could be better. She was a person living by her wits for many years, and she watched the news for clues. Local judges, politicians and the police forces were well known to Lizzie. She knew them, because many of them were, from time to time, her customers. It is no accident that Lizzie hired one of the top legal firms in Akron – Grant & the Honorable Judge George W. Sieber, as her attorneys. As with Lorenzo D. Watters, she chose her lawyers for the Winn litigation, with greater wisdom than she chose her husbands. Lorenzo himself might well have recused himself and recommended Grant & Sieber, during his third re-election to the mayor's office. One has to wonder if Arville's odd trust fund at the White Pigeon may have been the reason that the Winn trial fizzled out so quickly in Marion. Under the inexplicable trust fund, Lizzie could defend her maintenance of the White Pigeon as her sole source of child support for Arville. It defies logic, but the mayor of Akron was shepherding this trust. That would have carried weight with judges and other lawyers. Lizzie looked just marginally innocent, with Dan Fritz at the helm.

The New Year 1896 included a milestone in Lizzie's life, because her son Arville turned 18. Until then, it was Lorenzo D. Watters' responsibility to educate and support him out of proceeds from the White Pigeon. Arville had been a student living at 206 North Howard in Akron in 1894, living apart from his mother and her then husband – Jack "J.C." DeWitt, who resided up the North

Hill at 618 North Howard. Lorenzo was apparently keeping his end of the deal and overseeing Arville's care and education during this turbulent time in Lizzie's life.

The evidence that Lorenzo did indeed see to the education of Lizzie's young son Arville was a single textbook, <u>Commercial Law</u>.[77] It was kept by Arville's son, then by Arville's grandson and now by Arville's great-granddaughter – me. Did Lorenzo spend time with the boy and encourage him to try his hand at a legal education? Lorenzo came from humble roots in Lancaster, Ohio and was a self-made man. Arville may have emulated him and adored him. Or, did Lizzie encourage Arville to train in this field, because she could use legal help with her business? Or a third possibility – did Arville decide that he wanted an education in this field because of the bizarre trust that tied him to the rail of the White Pigeon until he reached his maturity at 25 years of age in 1903? That 1890 trust was ordered to stay in place for an additional *13 years* of Arville's life. It must have felt like a life sentence to an 18-year-old who saw his inheritance nearly blown away due to the Winn Law threat. The White Pigeon was a feathered noose around Arville's neck.

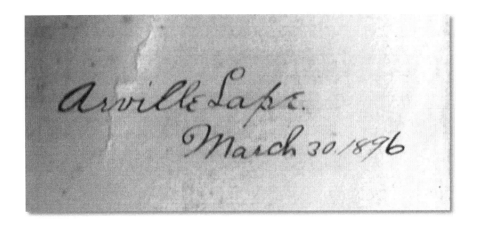

Illustrated Summit County, Ohio, 1891; Akron Map & Atlas Co.[78]

Hammel's Business College in Akron, Ohio – Akron-Summit County Public Library – Special Collections[79]

Henry Arville Lape [80]

Arville lost his legal guardian and mentor, Lorenzo Dow Watters, on September 27, 1896, reported the *Akron Beacon Journal*, when the three-term Mayor of Akron passed away following a long illness. He was a staunch Democrat, devoted husband and son. He died at his mother's home in Akron. His obituary summed up his character: *"He was thoroughly democratic in all his ways, and ever had for the humblest the same pleasant word to which he addressed to greater and more influential men."*

I would like to think Arville and Lizzie mourned this man of character, who helped shape our present day family.

CHAPTER 30

If It's a Girl Let's Name Her Bill

William Jennings Bryan[81]

1896 was a year of transition for 18-year old Arville. It was also a year of change for the nation, with the U.S. Presidential election coming up in November. The Democratic Party's candidate was William Jennings Bryan widely known as "the Great Commoner" by his populist followers. His opponent was William McKinley, a powerful player in the Ohio Republican party. William Jennings Bryan was born in southern Indiana but had traditional Old South political values inherited from his paternal Bryan family having roots in Virginia, Tennessee, and even Lizzie's state of Kentucky.[82] Jennings Bryan's father was Scottish-Irish and his religion was at various times Methodist, Baptist, Presbyterian, but at all times Protestant. Lizzie Rogers of Kentucky, could say the same.

In order to win the election, Bryan knew he had to win Ohio. He began what historians describe as the first stump speech campaign tour, travelling cross-country by train.[83] He was a powerful speaker and charismatic individual, attributes not lost on his audiences. He visited more train stations and depots than Lizzie, and was photographed campaigning in countless rural Ohio communities.[84] Bryan understood the advantages of taking the campaign to the people – that being essential to his populist message.

There were at least two people in Ohio who voted for William Jennings Bryan, one in fact, the other nominally, since women did not yet have the right to vote, namely Mr. and Mrs. Charles W. Veon. It might have seemed odd that avid saloonists such as Lizzie and Charles would support a prohibitionist-leaning politician. In 1896, however, Bryan was still riding the fence. He was, in fact, a late-comer to the prohibition table. According to a *New York Times* article in April 1918, Bryan had little taste for legislating temperance:

> ANTI-SALOON LEAGUE REPUDIATES BRYAN; Superintendent Anderson Says Nebraskan's Conversion Was Based on Hope for 1920. ATTACKS 'DRY FEDERATION' Declares Commoner Was Slower Changing Attitude Than Getting Onto American Side of War.[85]

Superintendent Anderson was further quoted as saying, "Mr. Bryan is frankly a joke so far as the Prohibition movement is concerned." This was hardly a surprise because as a populist Democrat, Bryan's constituents of commoners were the very people partaking of and making a living in the trade. His leanings were always in favor of the free will of the common man. Temperance, a choice that good men would freely make, was Bryan's original concept. This would have made perfect sense to free-enterprising Lizzie and Charles.

The Great Commoner never won the Presidency, despite three tries, and, although Bryan later defected to the prohibitionist cause, Lizzie probably remained a supporter, because Bryan helped ratify the 19th Amendment to the Constitution of the United States which prohibited state and local governments from denying any citizen the right to vote, based on that citizen's sex. Suffrage for women became the law of Lizzie's land on August 18, 1920.

Proof that Charles and Lizzie supported **and voted** for William Jennings Bryan in 1896: the Veons named their baby daughter after him. "Mary Jennings Bryan Veon", Arville Lape's half-sister, was born on December 3, 1896 in Stow, Ohio, one month to the day after William Jennings Bryan lost the election to Canton, Ohio's William McKinley. Little Mary Veon would not see a Democrat in the White House until after she was grown up and married.

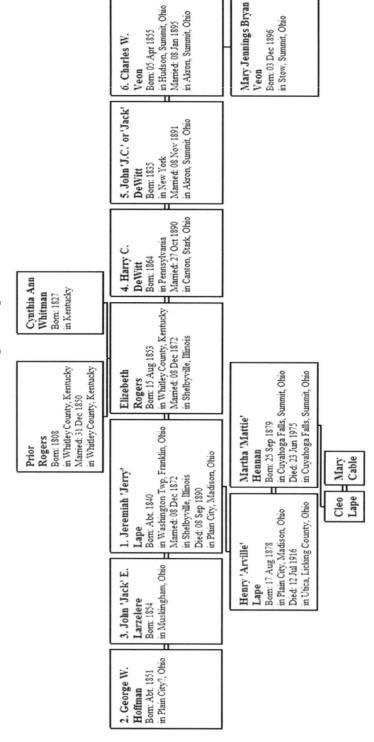

Lizzie's Tree - grows again

CHAPTER 31

Familiar Terrain

On May 21, 2009, I headed out to Stow, Ohio. It was to be a scorcher according to Cleveland TV. I'd come prepared with bottled water, camera, and printouts of Google.com and Bing.com maps. Only my husband knew I was planning to visit Stow to look for Lizzie. If I discovered something interesting, then I'd have an attentive audience. But without a lucky strike, my incessant chatter about Lizzie was as popular as a miner 49'er discussing his hopes for hitting the mother lode. No sense wearing out my audience.

I arrived in Stow before 8 am intending to devote the day to discovering anything about Gorge House aka Cliff House. The previous week, I had spent a day at the Main Branch of the Summit County Library in Akron, finding dozens of articles about Lizzie and her activities in and around the city. But it was not her activities there that excited me so much as three articles from 1898 concerning a property in Stow Corners named Cliff House, owned at one time by General Gross and Mr. and Mrs. Kidney. That's the day I *knew* with certainty that Lizzie had owned the property 112 years earlier known as Cliff or Gorge House pictured in the lithograph that I had purchased over 20 years before. Until that moment, Gorge House was just an interesting lithograph, not an important family memento.

Knowing Gorge House had been in the family made me impatient to visit my ancestral – er – home. I had to visit Stow, and soon. Without an actual land records map, it dawned on me that an aerial map would show the gorge itself. According the clippings, the inn was near the gorge.

Bing.com maps revealed the gorge in an autumn photograph to be one rocky mass of enormous proportion. However, the gorge abutted at least three roads that I could identify from the map, one of which was specifically named, Gorge

Park Rd. Arriving in Stow that morning, I didn't know where to start. Pulling into a gas station, I paused to figure out which way to begin.

That's when my cell phone rang. For one other-worldly moment, I fantasized it was Lizzie calling with guidance – "Hello time-traveling Great-Granddaughter. You've come this far, I guess I'll have to show you the rest of the way to that place we called home." It wasn't Lizzie of course, it was my mother on the other end of the telephone line with directions.

Mom had been a young college student dating my dad at Kent State University. Many times after school, she traveled with him and studied in the library in Akron while Dad finished up his night job there. Then he would drive her home. They traveled between Kent, Akron and Cleveland on these study/work days. After Mom and Dad married, she traveled with Dad's family for an occasional Sunday dinner out. One of Dad's family members, Martha, took a special liking to my mom, the same Martha – Dad's grandmother – who became my great-grandmother, Martha "Mattie" Atherholt.

Mom had awakened that morning in May 2009, recalling something she thought might be helpful. She did not know I was sitting in Stow facing the gorge. She said, "I remembered something that Grandma Atherholt told me when we drove through Stow in the 50's, and I thought it might be helpful. Now, let's see if I can explain where to go. When we'd drive from Kent into Stow, at the main intersection in Stow, we'd sometimes turn left going south." That was precisely the intersection and direction in which my car faced. "Once you are just past the business intersection, there are three houses on the right. Grandma said she lived in one of those houses when she was young." I needed clarification. "Don't you mean where Lizzie lived, not Martha?" I asked, suddenly confused. "No", she said, "Where *Martha* lived".

I drove just beyond the business district and there in relative isolation were three houses on my right, as Mom described. And all three buildings were perched on the rim of the gorge itself.

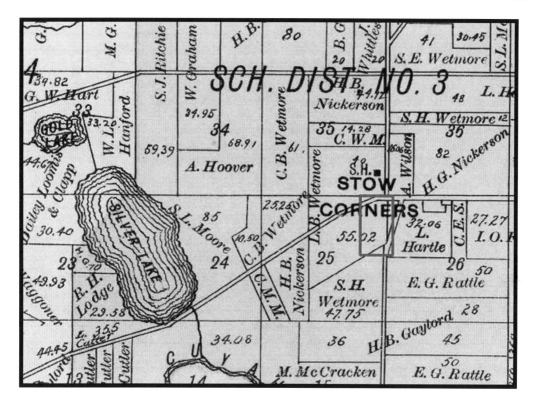

Summit County Atlas Map [86]
(red box is Cliff House property)

136 • LOOKING FOR LIZZIE

1874 Summit County Atlas – lithograph of Gorge House aka Cliff House, Stow Corners, O.[87]

With her perfectly-timed phone call, Mom added a new update to the meager oral tradition surrounding Lizzie. It had never really occurred to Mom or to me, that Mattie might have lived with her mother-in-law Lizzie in Stow. Now *that* was a new line of thought to pursue. Could there have been *two* madams in the family? Why not? Arville had to have met and fallen in love with Martha in this vicinity since they were married in Stow Corners. That is, at least *one* of their wedding ceremonies was performed there.

The early morning moment with Mom on the phone, was one of those serendipitous thrills. A synonym for the word "serendipity" is "happy accident". But Mom – calling me on the phone – there, that day, that way – was no accident. It was downright uncanny. If Lizzie had wanted to send directions, she couldn't have found a better messenger.

I stopped that day at the three houses perched on the rim of the gorge, taking pictures and soaking in the scenes from the top of the cliff and below in the gorge itself, with grottos where water gurgled to form deep, dark, mesmerizing pools of intricately worn bowls of stone. Ferns poked out lush and verdant in the dappled sunlight. It was and still is a natural paradise, a lyrical secret garden, accompanied by the music of falling water. My own memory of another place leapt to mind. The idyllic lush corner of Stow reminded me of another grander waterfall in paradise – one I'd visited recently from Lizzie's distant past – Cumberland Falls, Whitley County, Kentucky.

I knew then, why word of this place managed to make it through our family oral history of five generations. And I suspected too, why this place in Stow Corners meant more to Lizzie than all of the other places she bought and sold throughout her life. Simply put, it reminded her of home.

The Gorge at Stow, Ohio

CHAPTER 32

An Orphan with the Luck of the Irish

Lizzie's baby Mary Veon was born in Stow, Ohio, in December, 1896. Stow Township was well known by Charles and his parents Robert and Ellen Veon who lived there earlier and were significant landowners. Perhaps Lizzie and Charles rented a place in Stow in 1896. In the Akron Business Directory, they were still listed at 206 North Howard as residence and 184 S. Howard for the sample room and restaurant, but by the 1897 Directory compilation they had moved from Akron.

In early 1897, Lizzie purchased Cliff House and its surrounding ten acres from Charles and Elsie Kidney for $2,000. Of note, Lizzie's husband's name did not appear on the deed. It looks as if Charles made a trade with Elsie Kidney for land he previously owned in Portage County to complete funding of the acquisition of Lizzie's new place. The rest of the transaction was mortgaged. Perhaps Cliff House was Charles' gift to Lizzie upon the birth of their daughter Mary.

While Lizzie was making her plans and land transactions in March, there was love elsewhere in the air. Son Henry Arville, had fallen in love with a beautiful young woman named Martha "Mattie" Hennan. In 1896 Mattie lived and worked in Akron while Arville was working on his studies at Hammel's Business College. And in May of that same year, Mattie's 32-year-old mother Alice died of typhoid malaria, leaving Mattie destitute and alone in the city to fend for herself.

Mattie's story was complicated and tragic. When she was less than four years old, her mother Alice Shannon gave her up for adoption because Mattie's father had abandoned both the mother and daughter following the death of Mattie's baby brother Clarence. Her father was described in the adoption records as a drunkard, and had enlisted as a young cavalryman during the Spanish American War. Mattie was adopted by the Barrett family, but the adoption was terminated when the adoptive father died young and Mattie was returned to her impoverished mother Alice.

It is hard to understand the desperation that makes a young mother give up a child for adoption, but one fact was clear – at the beginning of the 20th century women made up less than 20% of the workforce. There were very few legitimate jobs for women and fewer still that paid a living wage. Alice made her choices. Lizzie made other choices.

The dime store where Mattie worked was just a few blocks from Lizzie and Charles' sample rooms and restaurant. They may have known each other in passing. It was a lively city filled with beautiful theaters, music and dance halls, new hotels and the new Buchtel College where Mattie's mother Alice had worked, cooking and cleaning. In 1896, following Alice's death, Mattie was on her own and living in the city in rented rooms. She was just sixteen years old.

Mattie Hennan Lape Atherholt (1879 – 1975) [88]

Assuming that Mattie and Arville were like Akron canal boats that passed in the night, the young lovers may not have been introduced until Lizzie hired a married couple, Richard and Lilly Underwood of Cuyahoga Falls, to run Cliff House. "Dick" Underwood was to be the bartender/bouncer and we can only speculate what Lilly's job was to be at Cliff House. The parallels between the Dan and Mattie Fritz team at the White Pigeon and the Dick and Lilly Underwood team at Cliff House were striking.

Mattie herself was not likely to have been one of the "faint doves" or "inmates" as the newspapers liked to describe the prostitutes that worked at Lizzie's places. No, Mattie was more probably hired to help with housekeeping at Cliff House. You see, Lilly Underwood's sister was Alice Shannon, and Mattie was therefore, her orphaned 16-year-old niece, come to live and work at Cliff House.

Alice Shannon Hennan (Mattie's mother) (1863 – 1896) [89]

CHAPTER 33

Two Baptisms, One Wedding & [Almost] a Funeral

I wonder what Cliff House looked like on the day that Mattie and Arville married there? It wasn't a shotgun wedding, unlike Mattie's mother's wedding. Alice had been five months pregnant with Mattie at the time. No, this was a happy day for Arville, Mattie and all of Arville's family. Even Mattie's grandfather, Robert O. Shannon, had arrived for this special day. Mattie's Aunt Lilly and Uncle Dick were there, naturally. Cliff House was probably the most highly decorated it had been since old General Gross, the original hotel proprietor, saw to the party planning and entertainment. The walks and lawns would have been trimmed and swept, with spring flowers and ferns blooming. Perhaps the bride carried Lily of the Valley from the garden.

In her line of work, Lizzie knew how to throw a party. This would have been a very special occasion for her. The White Pigeon in Marion was in operation and her son would soon take charge there. He had studied bookkeeping and business law, with the help of the Mayor of Akron. Arville knew the business – he'd grown up in it, as so many children of his generation. At 19, he was young for marriage, but Lizzie had been the same age herself when she married Jeremiah. By that time, she was worldly beyond her years. But these were modern times, not war years, and Lizzie was hopeful for many reasons, not least of which was that Mattie was a sweet child.

For Lizzie, Mattie was the wife she would have wished for her son – an innocent, kind-hearted girl. In her line of work, Lizzie of necessity had either forgone or given up babies for adoption or abortion earlier in her life. Certainly, there had been other children Lizzie had lost – five in all, two living, as she would reveal to a later census taker. Mattie was a good girl and Arville was lucky to have found her. Mattie was also a step up on the social ladder, as so many doors would obviously have been closed to Lizzie. But what brought and kept Lizzie and Mattie close was their shared sad beginnings. Mattie had experienced much loss in her young life. Lizzie would do everything that she could for Mattie, as she had for Arville.

Now this may sound a bit ridiculous, when you consider what young Arville had managed to survive at Lizzie's hand – five stepfathers and more than a few homes shared with the "inmates". Yet Lizzie was a survivor, even if a cliff-hanger. When she could afford to let go of one hand on the rung of life, she extended it to her family. She was a generous woman, and perhaps most astonishingly – a romantic.

The wedding certificate of Arville Lape and Mattie Hennan in Stow Corners, discovered in Mattie's papers after her death.[90]

As with all 20-20 visions of the past, this one needed a slight correction. Rose-colored glasses aside, the full truth about events that day at Cliff House is contained within the records of St. John's Episcopal Church in Cuyahoga Falls.

Photo Courtesy of St. John's Episcopal Church, Cuyahoga Falls, Ohio[1]

The same Reverend Robert Kell, who took the time to travel to Cliff House and perform the marriage service for Arville and Mattie, performed two other church services that day at Cliff House. Lizzie and her baby daughter Mary were baptized together at home, while the wedding couple looked on as sponsors with the bride's aunt, Lilly Underwood.

Conspicuously absent from the list of witnesses for the wedding or the baptisms was Charles Veon, Lizzie's husband. Part of the explanation as to why Lizzie chose to be baptized on this day, may be recorded in Rev. Kell's notes next to Lizzie's name in his St. John's book of baptisms – "At Stow Corners Hotel. Sick."

There might have been a little immortal soul-searching by Lizzie as she lay sick at home. Perhaps she had not recovered well from the late-in-life birth of Mary Veon. Women died in childbirth frequently; at age 43 the odds increased. It was clear that her new daughter-in-law Mattie was enthusiastic at Lizzie's joining the church; she was listed as witness on both Mary's and Lizzie's baptisms. Arville's bride was trying to look out for the best interests of her new mother-in-law and baby sister-in-law, the best way she knew how. There were few women in Lizzie's personal life until Mary, Mattie, and Lilly came along. The companionship of these women was a welcome change.

CHAPTER 34

A Chance to Make a Mint of Money

Meanwhile... back at the White Pigeon, things were running off the rails. The Pigeon was in the news again, making comedic and ominous *Marion Daily Star* headlines, in the same edition. On March 24, 1897, the paper ran two reports, one to entertain the masses headlined with "SHE LOST HER FURS"; the other titled "DOOMED" seemed to be aimed at a readership of a growing number of citizen reformers who were ready for a change.

"SHE LOST HER FURS" is a Keystone Cop confection of dizzying claims by "inmates" of unfair treatment at the hands of each other and by the landlord "Manager Veon". Perhaps Charles? If so, it sounds as if the place was running amok under his supervision. The subtitle was "The Late Cook at the White Pigeon Makes a Charge", which is really hard to do, especially if you are deceased. Setting aside the blooper subtitle, the whole story is a lulu. Seems the cook had her furs stolen by a couple of the resident workers who were behind in paying Manager Veon for their board bills. They secretly loaded up one trunk and left two empties as collateral with Manager Veon. The cook went to the police station but was told the paperwork would take time, whereupon the cook decided to skip the niceties and pursue the purloined furs to Dayton, herself.

The second article titled "DOOMED" about sums it up:

> "Doomed Is the White Pigeon, Which May Be Wiped Out of Existence."
>
> "The proprietor Charles Veon who is the husband of Lizzie Lape-Lazalere-DeWitt, will still run the saloon, but the house connected

> there will soon be run by other people. Mrs. Veon has leased the house. The majority of the frail doves who inhabited the place are leaving the city."

With the dawn of 1897, Lizzie quit Marion for her new home in Stow. She leased the house and left Charles in charge of the Pigeon's saloon. But Lizzie couldn't really abandon the White Pigeon completely because it was Arville's inheritance. It was a 118-mile conundrum; 236 miles round trip. Trains helped, but it was not possible to commute daily.

On May 4th, the following headline ran in the papers:

> POLICE MAKE RAID –
>
> "The White Pigeon Visited at an Early Hour This Morning".
>
> "They went early and stayed late, and were making the night hideous about the place".

The Marion police force took a vote and decided that they didn't like Lizzie's replacement, Nellie Burk. That is to say, they raided the house soon after Lizzie left town. And although the resort was apparently attracting a "better crowd" under the new management, the sheer volume of the flock was disturbing the neighborhood.

This harks back to earlier notoriety in the 1886 *Marion Daily Star* when Lizzie came to town and was quoted as "playing to a full house". Even more illustrative, "Hiding places were at a premium, and in their attempts to conceal themselves ostriches might have done better..." What a vivid picture this *Marion Star* reporter painted of the scene at the Pigeon! It was chaos and bedlam and this article would sell papers for Warren G. Harding. It's a lighthearted romp, a confection worthy of Mark Twain. Laughter cures us of too heavy a judgment upon these souls, as they are made ridiculous instead of evil. The secret ingredient was the common cackle.

MAY 4, 1897.

POLICE MAKE A RAID

"WHITE PIGEON" VISITED AT AN EARLY HOUR THIS MORNING

Seven Unmentionables, Two Females and One Young Man Were Caught and Compelled To Produce--Two Females and Several Unmentionables Got Away.

The White Pigeon's feathers were ruffled by the police officers at an early hour this morning. The occasion was the most exciting and sensational that resort has ever experienced. Some time since a Mrs. Veon leased the house to Nellie Burk, a woman who bore a bad name at Bucyrus, and whom it is said was compelled to leave that place. Since she came to Marion and assumed charge of the White Pigeon prosperity seemed to come to that place. It had become a resort where the so-called better classes visited.

Monday night crowds visited the disreputable place in swarms. They went early and stayed late, and were making night hideous about the premises when Marshal Blain and the entire police force made their raid. Twenty-five is the estimate placed on the number of souls in the house at the time. The officers surrounded the house and made a grand and unexpected rush, but many escaped. Two females and seven unmentionable visitors were captured. Two females and several other unmentionable visitors got away.

> When the officers rushed through the doors there was a lively scramble. Hiding places were at a premium, and in their attempts to conceal themselves ostriches might have done better than some of the men. Some crowded behind trunks, back of clothing on the walls and others secreted themselves under beds.
>
> Marshal Blain lined up his catch and compelled the men to put up ten dollars each for their appearance at 8 o'clock. Nellie Bush, the landlady, put up twenty-five dollars and May Ford, the other female captured, deposited ten dollars, and promised to appear this afternoon at 1 o'clock. Arthur Lape, the bartender, put up for his appearance, and came into court at 8 o'clock this morning and had his case continued until 1 o'clock this afternoon.
>
> The unmentionables gave their names as Thomas Smith, William Lake, Richard Johnson, Theodore Miller, John Brown, Arthur French and Thos Ferguson. They have not appeared in police court. They are not expected. They will likely remain incog
>
> This afternoon Lape came up and pleaded guilty to the charge of being in a house of ill repute, and was fined ten dollars and costs.

Marion Daily Star – May 4, 1897[91]

Here for the first time, was Arville identified in the news of the White Pigeon. Now that he was taking an active role, he was fair game.

On May 5, 1897, the day after the big raid, the *Star* ran an article titled "MUST GO". Nellie Burk/Bush, the out-of-towner who leased the house from Lizzie, was told to leave town or face the workhouse in Columbus, Ohio.

The mood was mixed with the *Marion Daily Star* readership. Some wanted reform; others wanted things as they were; while still others just wanted to make a living. Not an easy thing if you were a woman. By 1897, it was clear to many impoverished young women that there was fast money to be made in houses of ill-repute. Within 10 years, Floradora Girls and Evelyn Nesbit on that red velvet swing would glamorize this storyline. Prostitution was and still is a money maker, most of it, brutally unglamorous. But there was more going on at that time in America to draw participants. What caused hundreds, no thousands of young women across America to run away from their straight and narrow lives and veer off track to a freedom of their own, as risky as it was? The Nellie Burks and May Fords of the world didn't want to work at places like Lizzie's – they wanted to *be* a Lizzie, managing their own stylish house, hosting glittering soirees for the rich and the powerful, owning their own property – being in every way in control of their own destiny. Heady stuff, for a burgeoning population of lower middle class women long considered chattels themselves. Emulation was the sincerest form of flattery, even for a lady of the evening.

Between May and October, we might assume that Lizzie did her best to find a suitable replacement for Nellie Burk, her sub-lessee and resident Madam at the White Pigeon. Arville's mother may have decided that the mood in Marion was too hot for her young son and his new wife to run the White Pigeon saloon *and* the bawdy house next door. Officer Blain was riding a wave of missionary zeal against vice.

In this interim period, Lizzie and Charles leased another saloon on the opposite side of the depot, north of town. It was less than a mile from the Pigeon as the crow flies, but much farther by roadway, due to the volume of industry and train traffic that existed there at the Big Four depot, known as the Cleveland, Cincinnati, Chicago and St. Louis Railway after their merger in 1889. To early train historians, Marion was the Mecca for railroaders because it was the converging point for many rail lines.

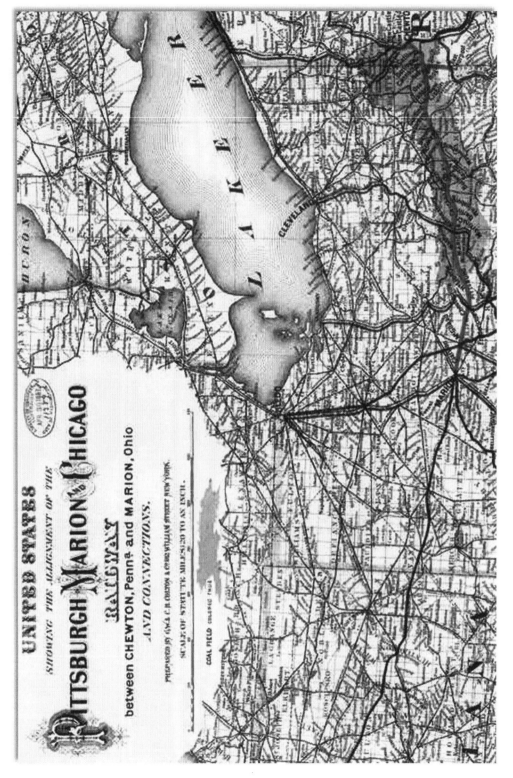

1887 early railway map showing significance of Marion, Ohio railroad hub[92]

The location of Lizzie's new saloon was significant. She chose not to locate too close to the White Pigeon, probably because she did not want to compete directly with her son. Her new place on Kenton Ave. was a saloon which did not appear to have an adjacent bawdy house, although there was apparently a boarding house conveniently located across the street – possibly to evade the Winn Law. It is not known if Lizzie had a business interest in that "boarding" house.

Arville and Mattie had made the move to Marion, where Arville was managing the White Pigeon – at least the saloon/bar portion of the business. Lizzie lent a hand to launch the new White Pigeon under Arville's management, appearing for the first time on the scene acting as hostess at the Pigeon's 4-star buffet. The four stars were the ones circling the head of an ill-mannered guest rude enough to stick his fingers in the buffet dishes, whereupon Lizzie took aim and clobbered him with a dish:

> "A patron at the White Pigeon, while under the influence of squirrel whisky, amused himself by sticking his fingers in the dishes. Lizzie Veon, the madam, struck him over the head with a plate, and the bartender afterwards gave him a severe beating and further punishment. [Lizzie's son Arville, perhaps?] Officer Murphy was called and brought the fellow to the city prison, but he was afterwards released. The proprietor of the house was not arrested."

Marion Daily Star – Oct. 2, 1897 [93]

What follows were the first signs of discord between Arville and step-father Charles W. Veon in the *Star*.

> **TROUBLE**
> **Comes from the White Pigeon Saloon to Justice's Court.**
>
> Some time ago Arville Lape, the son of Lizzie Lape-Lazalere-Veon, purchased the saloon of his step-father, C. W. Veon, but since that time Veon has remained most of the time about the house. He seems to like the place and is in no hurry to leave. The one thing that he retains is a cash register, and by the terms of the agreement can not take it away.
>
> Young Arville Lape, however, is desirous of having this to complete his little grog shop that stands near the "white pigeon" structure proper, and as he alleges that C. W. Veon is indebted to him in the amount of $77 he has brought suit in the court of 'Squire Gompf to recover the amount, and has issued an attachment on the cash register. Young Lape explains that there is a chance to make a mint of money out of the place, but that Veon is ruining all chances of money-making.

Marion Daily Star – Nov. 18, 1897 [94]

The article suggests that Arville bought out the saloon business, but this may have been erroneous and had more to do with the White Pigeon trust between Lizzie and Arville. There was no evidence that Charles ever owned the White Pigeon.

Arville was having a devilish time getting his step-father to vacate the premises so that he could run his "little grog shop that stands near the White Pigeon structure proper." This was the most complete explanation of the layout on the property – a bawdy house called the White Pigeon and a separate building on the property that housed the saloon.

Arville got his hearing before the bench, turning his recent *Commercial Law* training into action.

> "Constable Mack this afternoon sold the cash register at the White Pigeon. It was sold to secure money due on an attachment suit brought by Orville Lape against Charles and Elizabeth Veon."

Marion Daily Star – Dec. 6, 1897 [95]

It would seem that Arville won his case against his step father and, according to the article, his own mother. If Arville included his mother Lizzie in the suit, it wouldn't have been a big surprise, considering the litigious nature of this family.

CHAPTER 35

We'll Leave the [Red] Light On for You

Lizzie had plenty of experience elsewhere, but could she make a success of her seen-better days "hotel" and saloon in Stow? While Arville and Mattie were setting up housekeeping at the White Pigeon in Marion, the new old place in Stow was becoming a hot spot. Trouble was afoot at Cliff House, as most of Summit County apparently suspected. Since the Veons were following Lizzie's usual *modus operandi*, the reformers and the vice patrol including the "Winn-Fall" activists, assumed rightly or wrongly that they had found a new bawdy house/saloon to target. The full weight of the Winn Law fell on Lizzie's Cliff House, starting even before the two baptisms and a wedding. The 1897 *Akron Beacon Journal Index* read like a rap sheet.

In August, Lizzie and Charles were arrested and Charles was held in Summit County jail overnight, while Lizzie was released. She did not come to the jail to post bail for Charles. Instead, Charles' father Robert Veon paid the $200 and retrieved his son. Again in October, Charles was arrested, found guilty, and released after serving one day in jail.

Some person or persons in Stow were determined to drive Lizzie and her business out of town. Lizzie had big plans for her place in Stow Corners. Stow was and still is to this day, a green oasis in a sea of cityscapes. The gorge behind Cliff House with its tinkling waterfalls and bubbling brooks was so like Cumberland Falls, Kentucky, Lizzie's homeland. She chose to hold a wedding for her son there, and have her baby and herself baptized in Stow. She was emotionally invested in Stow Corners. And too, she had a business vision for Cliff House that she wasn't about to give up readily… even if her husband was.

After the arrests in Stow, he made a point of spending more time in Marion than Stow. His drinking habit of old resurfaced, he was making a nuisance of himself at the White Pigeon, and generally becoming a problem for Lizzie as well as Arville.

After the events of late '97, things at Stow Corners would have to cool down before Lizzie could proceed with plans there. In hers and Charles' extended absences, Mattie's aunt and uncle – Dick and Lilly Underwood, were hired to fill in for the Veons at the Stow hotel as caretakers.

By 1898 Lizzie's family ran three saloons, two in Marion plus Cliff House in Stow. Operating these watering holes meant a steady flow of activity with beer and liquor suppliers, grocery and food providers, and hired help including cooks, maids, cleaning staff, property maintenance and livery. That was the front door traffic of saloon business. However, due to the increased societal pressure, there was more and more back door traffic to contend with, if a saloonist were to keep himself out of debtors' prison. Payoffs and rake offs were common.[96]

Lizzie and Arville opened their saloon doors to a tremendous swath of humanity. To think about the scoundrels and wastrels, hacks and editors, lawyers and politicians, actors and quacks, the newest ideas and older schemes, and the comedic banter that they were witness to – is a marvel. It had to be a lively lesson in all that is human. That was the saloon at the turn of the last century. For better or worse.

Any place where *"I'll have my usual"* is answered by a friendly smile from the hostess or knowing nod from the bartender is a destination worth seeking, then and now. That was the "welcome" sign that made the saloon a second home to many tired, lonely people – of all spheres. It was an experiment in Democracy that worked. My family was in the hospitality business before Prohibition. It wasn't an evil way of life; it was an American institution.

Weber's – in operation since 1902
51 West Main Street, Shelby Ohio

CHAPTER 36

Someone Lit a Match in a Dry Town

1898 was an important year for Arville and Mattie, because they had a baby son, a first grandchild for Lizzie. Into this family of quixotic characters from a Victorian morality play, my grandfather Cleo, was born. Four days before his birth, his great-uncle Dick Underwood was hauled off to jail for selling liquor illegally in Stow. Cliff House was back in the papers.

> **For Selling Intoxicants.**
>
> Richard Underwood, proprietor of the Cliff house at Stow Corners, is in trouble for the alleged selling of intoxicating liquor in a "dry" township.
>
> Wednesday he was given a hearing before 'Squire C. N. Gaylord, of Stow, where he pleaded not guilty. The evidence against him is said to be very strong, and he was bound over to the common pleas court in the sum of $300. W. W. Richardson, the horseman, living a short distance below Butler' Corners, furnished the required bail.

Akron Beacon Journal – August 20, 1898 [97]

Same trouble/different bartender – this time Dick Underwood instead of Charles Veon. Even the same judge – Squire Gaylord of Stow. Lizzie and Charles did not post bail for their bartender, who was also their new daughter-in-law's uncle. There follows another article in the *Akron Beacon Journal*, September 20, 1898 edition detailing Dick Underwood's plea of guilty and fine of $75 for serving liquor in dry Stow Corners.

Then on October 6, 1898, the *Journal* reported:

Mrs. Veon Objects to Selling Liquor on Her Property [98]

Within four days of Dick Underwood's arrest, Lizzie was reportedly suing Mattie's aunt and uncle for selling liquor on her property in Stow and refusing to vacate Cliff House.

Poor souls, they probably never knew what hit them – Hurricane Lizzie was on the move, probably upon the advice of her savvy Akron lawyers. Having just avoided prosecution in Marion on the Winn Law, Lizzie was well-versed in the need to distance herself as property owner from the individuals she hired to sell liquor on her property in a dry town. For Lizzie, property ownership came first ahead of familial ties to the Underwood family – Mattie's family. It was not a pretty story.

Cracks in family solidarity started to form, just as they had in so many other incarnations of Lizzie's past "families". This time, she was 45-years old with an infant grandson, a two-year old daughter, an 18-year old daughter-in-law, a 20-year old son, and a 43-year old husband (#6) – with a growing drinking problem.

It had to be a difficult time for Lizzie, who had once again chosen a husband weaker than her in many ways. 1899 started out with a bang. On January 10th, the *Akron Beacon Journal* edition reported Lizzie's lawsuit against the Treasurer of Summit County which was prompted by Treasurer Miles' advertising Cliff House for sale due to short payment on the Dow Tax assessed for 1897. As she had bought the place in March, 1897, it should have been an easy case to prove or disprove. Since the Treasurer was enjoined from selling the property and since there was no follow up we can assume Lizzie won this battle.

Meanwhile back in Marion, the *Daily Star* reported on Feb. 3, 1899 that a jury of her peers had reached an impasse in Squire Gomph's court on a claim between Lizzie and creditor named "Shields". And on May 8th, another creditor suit brought to the Marion court by George Lang "and others", succeeded in a judgment against Lizzie.

But the clincher was this one from the *Akron Daily Democrat*, May 27, 1899 [99] edition, not a headliner, but one that underscored Lizzie's woes...

> Chas. ▓▓▓ and H. J. Hurbruck are registered as drunks.

These were the travails of Lizzie that made it to the papers circa 1899. She was falling into financial ruin in two different counties. But the worst was yet to come.

> **HOTEL BURNED,**
>
> **An Old Landmark at Stow Corners Gone.**
>
> The Stow Corners hotel, which was a land mark at that place and which for many years did a big business, but in late years fell into ill repute, burned at 2 o'clock, Friday morning. It was better known as "Kidney's."
> The fire is thought to be of an incendiary origin. The loss will be about $2,000.

Akron Beacon Journal – September 7, 1899 [100]

Stow Corners Hotel aka Cliff House aka Kidney Hotel *aka* Gorge House – Gone.

With the fire, Lizzie's big plans went up in smoke, then floated down into the lowest caverns of the Gorge, behind what once was – Cliff House.

Lizzie lost a lot that night. Her family pictures, personal belongings, business and legal documents, a home and a dream went up in flames. On Friday September 1st at two in the morning, someone had set the place ablaze. From the reports, no one died in this fire so it is a guess that Lizzie and her family were not in Stow that night. Probably, the family was at one of their two Marion venues. The paper mentions no suspects, and there were no subsequent reports in the Akron papers. Nobody, even the press, appeared interested in its "incendiary origins". The place had been branded a public nuisance.[101]

But, who was the arsonist? As with an old-fashioned murder mystery, there were plenty of suspects with motive. First suspect – the Stow townsfolk. They had to have been sick and tired of the shenanigans at the old Kidney Place, and it's likely that things didn't get better when Lizzie was out of town and the Underwoods were running the show. The good people of Stow had plenty of good reasons for wanting Lizzie to leave town.

To find someone with motivation to burn the place down, you could look a lot closer to Cliff House. Dick Underwood may well have harbored serious resentment for his treatment at the hands of Lizzie and Charles. They essentially hung him out to dry when he was arrested for selling liquor there.

Charles Veon too, may have been developing a growing resentment for the property, since Lizzie owned it, and he did not, and it may have been consuming her time and attention, at the expense of his own little grog shop.

> **Foreclosure.**
> Mrs. Jane S. Steinbacher has filed a petition in Common Pleas court asking that a mortgage she holds, given by Lizzie Veon, be foreclosed. The amount due is $1,000. The property covered by the mortgage is the old Kidney house at Stow Corners.

Akron Daily Democrat – Oct. 30, 1899 [102]

Another person with potential motivation was the mortgage holder Jane Steinbacher. It didn't take her long to file a foreclosure suit against Lizzie, once the house burned to the ground. To add fuel to this particular fire, there was a Major E. Steinbacher whose house had also been damaged by fire in 1895.

> ### To Foreclose a Mortgage.
>
> Jane E. Steinbacher has begun suit in Common Pleas court against Lizzie and Charles Veon, and Charles E. and Elsie R. Kidney, for the foreclosure of a mortgage held by the plaintiff on the property now occupied by the Veons. They bought the property of the Kidneys and assumed a $1,000 claim held by Mrs. Steinbacher on the property. The claim is in the form of a promissory note given October 20, 1894.

Akron Daily Democrat – Oct. 28, 1899 [103]

And of course, last but not least – there was Lizzie herself. She couldn't continue to run it as a saloon, because of the local "dry" ordinances, so it must have turned into a very poor investment. Lizzie held an insurance policy on the property. She could convert Cliff House into cash, if the place burned down. Cash was something Lizzie always needed, perhaps desperately so.

Take your pick. Somebody burned Cliff House down, on purpose.

CHAPTER 37

The Little Girl Who Saw Everything

For Lizzie, fire had to hold personal terror. She'd managed to escape the Chicago Fire of 1871, and she had been badly burned in the stove explosion in Akron. If someone were trying to scare Lizzie away, he or she could not have picked a more perfect nightmare for her.

She didn't linger in Stow. She very quickly bought a house in Marion, just 17 days after the fire, a few blocks from the White Pigeon. Was this Marion home for Arville and Mattie and grandson Cleo? It was perfectly located for a brief walk to the Pigeon, without actually being in its notorious west end neighborhood.

But Lizzie didn't linger long in Marion either. She was ready for a change. What took her to the next town? Was it word of a bigger train junction? A good deal on a property? A friend in law enforcement? Family troubles? A new man?

Or was she just being Lizzie? Perhaps she simply decided to start over. It was time. She didn't give up; she didn't slow down. It wasn't in her nature. Stow hadn't worked out, but Shelby might.

> Elizabeth Vcon, of Marion, has purchased the saloon and restaurant formerly conducted by Jacob Lewis.

Mansfield News, January 1, 1900. Brief News Notes [from Shelby, Ohio] [104]

On the first day of the 20th century, the *Mansfield News* announced that Lizzie had purchased Jacob Lewis' saloon and restaurant in Shelby. From the June, 1900 census, taken there we learn that Lewis House was located on North Broadway in Shelby, in Richland County, Ohio, about 42 miles NE of Marion.

Looking North on North Broadway. Lizzie's saloon and restaurant were on the west side of road, near where the road disappears in the distance.

The Big Four Depot, Shelby, Ohio – two doors from Lizzie's

Lizzie in classic madam form, purchased an existing bordello with a bad reputation, just as she had the White Pigeon, located along the railroad tracks. The house was within jumping-off distance of the newly built railroad junction.

Lizzie had located to a wild and free industrial boomtown poised to propel everyone there into the middle class. 112 years ago, Lizzie was back in business in a place that might not have been a green oasis, but was more disposed to her trade. All around, were boarding houses and saloons, since North Broadway was a thoroughfare between the new depot and the opera house and other attractions at the corner of North Broadway and Main. Traffic was brisk.

Shelby was also home to many new manufacturers, and even when the train wasn't passing, the clank and hum of industrial equipment could be heard throughout town. Shelby's industry required and attracted a large population of young men, eager to make a better living. It was hard, backbreaking, sweltering work in the shops. The life span of these men was undoubtedly shortened from exposure to solvents and chemicals used in metal plating processes, not to mention the risk to life and limb of the rolling mills. Men aged rapidly. Still, even older men who found their families struggling on failed farms made their way into the city for these jobs, because they paid a living wage. These workers were exactly the kind of customers Lizzie catered to. She would have probably done quite well out west during the gold rush, if she'd been born a little earlier. But there were plenty of boomtowns left in Ohio, and Shelby was one. Akron and Stow in particular had been too tight a corset. In Shelby, Lizzie had her trains – and by now you *know* she liked to get up and go. At the end of a long evening, she would fall asleep to the sound of night trains, rumbling and whistling like a tea kettle, through her backyard. It *felt* like the White Pigeon.

Lewis House was notorious under its previous ownership, but under Lizzie's management, no string of arrests, fines or Winn/Dow legal battles were reported in the papers, leading one to wonder if she had gone legit. Perhaps she worked hard to make the saloon and restaurant work, and only took on boarders who paid by the month, not the hour or evening.

One block north of Lizzie's Lewis House, two sisters lived in the upper half of a house at 121 ½ North Broadway. The older sister Orpha Sherman Steinbrueck owned the house and took in boarders and rented out a saloon downstairs, too. Orpha had the prime spot overlooking the train depot. Lizzie also had a "prime" spot overlooking the B&O train tracks from her back door.

Orpha was cut from the same cloth as Lizzie. She was divorced, chose to live her life in her own way, and may have run something more than a boarding house in her early days. She had a young daughter too, like Lizzie. These two hard-working older women with young children would have recognized in each other a kindred spirit even if they hadn't been neighbors. She also had a niece the same age as Lizzie's daughter Mary Veon, and she too lived in Shelby until 1903 when her mother died in what was suspected to be a botched abortion. The niece came to live permanently with her aunt in 1910, having run away from a cruel stepmother. An observant child, she was enthralled by the hustle bustle of the train yard; the rough and ready characters that passed by and through her aunt's neighborhood. She wrote about them in her journals and years later, as well known writer Dawn Powell, captured Lizzie's world better than any other.

I contacted Tim Page, Dawn's biographer who helped me get acquainted with the hard-working, hard-living, *striving* town that was Dawn's and Lizzie's, Shelby, Ohio. Everyone was 'up and away' in Shelby, that is to say – people wanted more and weren't afraid to grab for the brass ring. Dawn ultimately did what her heroines did in her novels *Dance Night* and *My Home Is Far Away*. She took a fast train out of town with very little money in her pocket and a big plan for making an exciting new life.[105] She was headed for the big-time, and she would find it in New York City's glittering literary circles. Except for her destination, the pattern is remarkably familiar to every young woman without means but with ambition, including Lizzie.

Tim put me in touch with two wonderful women who evoked a great deal more of Lizzie's/Dawn's world, Dawn's niece, Carol Warstler and Sally Maier, curator/historian at the Shelby Museum. Sally invited me to visit the museum where my husband Claude and I were engrossed in the amazing collection – everything from city directories and newspapers; turn-of-the-century salesman sample cases from the Shelby Spring Hinge Company; manikins in Victorian attire; photographs of the train station in Lizzie and Orpha's neighborhood; photographs of Dawn Powell with her high school class; and one unexpected find – a photo of Arville when he worked at the Shelby Seamless Tube Company.

Sally took us for a trip up North Broadway, where Dawn's Aunt Orpha lived and where Lizzie's house stood. There's nothing left but the lot itself, a common ending to most of Lizzie's ill-reputed houses. Sally asked us if we were hungry and proceeded to take us to the local saloon for a sandwich and a beer. The saloon was the real deal – Weber's Bar, vintage 1902 – in fact, a competitor of Lizzie's! The perfect ending to a perfect day in the land of Lizzie.

Carol Warstler, Dawn Powell's niece, filled me in on the loving and humorous individual that was her Aunt Dawn. She had many critics in her day; most crushing were the advisors who thought her characters too coarse, too unrefined. Dawn countered that she loved all of her characters, warts and all.[106] And that is one of the aspects that make her writing timeless. Meet Lizzie, a flawed character in a tough world, warts and all.

Dawn Powell's Shelby was Lizzie's stage. The little girl who lived in the same neighborhood captured the restless spirit of the town, the uneasy tug to move up and move on; and *grow* in the process. She drew on memory, to breathe life back into a world that danced for her, as a child. Her characters are so imperfectly real, they live on.

One of the characters portrayed in *Dance Night* was a young woman who – when abandoned by the man she loved – chose Lizzie's path in life, starting work at *Lizzie* Madison's sporting house. From that point in the narrative, the young woman becomes unseen and unheard from, cut off from her old friends and way of life. Everyone whispers, but there are only rumors. A friend calls her on the telephone, but is disconnected abruptly. The curtain drops on a life unknown by Dawn, but well-known by Lizzie. It was in fact the shady side of the street.

"...and I says no, it's a hotel ain't it, and she says, 'Some hotel', she says, "it's Lizzie Madison's, the biggest sporting house in town."– from **Dance Night**' by Dawn Powell [107]

Lizzie and daughter Mary Veon, photographed in Shelby, Ohio, about 1902

CHAPTER 38

Gone Fishin'

1900 U.S. Census – Lizzie counted twice in both Marion and Shelby, Ohio.

Lizzie and Mary Veon were counted twice in the 1900 U.S. federal census. (The true population count of the United States in 1900 was 76,212,168 6.) Whoever provided the details for Lizzie's family in Marion got a few other things wrong: Lizzie's age was reduced by three years, the month of her birth was wrong, she was listed as having been married for 30 years(!) and Arville's name was confused with her absent husband's name, Charles Veon. Arville's birth date wasn't even close – he was 21 at the time of this census, but he always looked younger than his age. Finally, Lizzie was born in Kentucky, not Ohio.

If the bartender in Marion was Arville Lape, then where was Charles W. Veon? According to the 1900 census Charles had moved north to Lorain, Ohio, and was living with his younger brother Harry and his sister-in-law Ella. The press confirmed what was expected all along, that the Veons were divorcing:

SUES FOR DIVORCE.

4-27-1900

Elizabeth Veon's Cause of Action Against Charles W. Veon.

Elizabeth Veon, by her attorneys, Skiles & Skiles and T. J. Green, has begun proceedings in probate court against Charles W. Veon, asking for divorce. The parties were married at Cuyahoga Falls in Summit county on July 14, 1865. There was born of the marriage May J. Veon, now aged 3 years.

The plaintiff alleges that since her marriage, and on or about Aug. 1, 1897, and at other times thereafter the defendant committed adultery with one Mamie Gardner, who then resided in Marion. That since that time the plaintiff and defendant have not lived together as man and wife and that the defendant now lives in the city of Lorain.

The plaintiff claims that she holds in her own right certain property in the state of Ohio as well as household goods. The plaintiff prays that the defendant may be barred from any and all interest in the property and that she may have the care and custody of the child. Further, that she may be given a divorce from her husband, and also for other relief.—Mansfield News.

Mrs. Veon lives in Shelby and operates the restaurant along the B. & O. track which she purchased from Jacob Lewis.

Mansfield News and Shelby Times – April 27, 1900 [108]

Lizzie hired top-drawer representation again. Her divorce lawyers were Skiles, Skiles & Green of Shelby (Senior partner W. W. Skiles, would be elected to Congress in 1901).

Lizzie charged Charles with adultery as early as 1897, just days before she refused to bail him out of jail for selling liquor in Stow. His father had to post bail. Note the mention of the Jacob Lewis restaurant purchase along the B&O rail line. On Sept. 11, 1900 Lizzie got her divorce from Charles while retaining custody of little Mary and all of Lizzie's "considerable" property.

There were other family members missing from the 1900 census: Mattie and Cleo, Lizzie's daughter-in-law and grandson. They didn't appear at the White Pigeon or the new home in Marion, either. Seems they had moved to Cuyahoga Falls and were living with Mattie's aunt Lilly and Uncle Dick Underwood and their daughter Minnie.

> Two divorce suits were begun in common pleas court Tuesday. The first was that of Mattie Lape vs. Arville Lape in which the plaintiff charges her husband with being a habitual drunkard. The couple were married in May, 1897, and they have one son. The wife wants absolute divorce, restoration to her maiden name.

Akron Beacon Journal – July 31, 1900 [109]

Mattie had initiated divorce proceedings against Arville as an adulterer and "habitual drunkard". Lizzie would have surely deplored this suit because it revealed her son's weakness for liquor – a flaw of which creditors in Marion could take note.

> **MARRIED IN STOW.**
> Mrs. Hattie Lape wants a divorce form Arrville Lape. They were married at Stow, May 23, 1897. She alleges that he has violated his vows by being unfaithful to her. She also charged him with habitual drunkenness.

Akron Daily Democrat – July 31, 1900 [110]

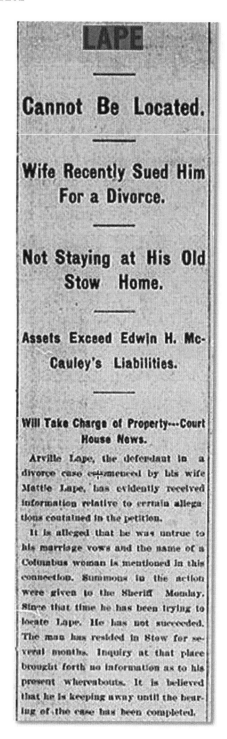

Akron Daily Democrat August 1, 1900 [111]

The Daily Democrat picked up this human interest story. Arville was living in Stow "for months" while trying to save his marriage, meaning he must have spent less time at the White Pigeon.

Stow was close to Cuyahoga Falls where Mattie and Cleo were living. Arville sought reconciliation, not a divorce from Mattie.

Akron Daily Democrat – August 9, 1900 [112]

One week later, the newspaper had the front page story scandal lovers were craving: Arville was caught living in a corn crib and fishing for bait, just east of Stow in Fish Creek. A corny big fish story... perfect bait for newspaper readers.

The Pflueger story was a tongue-in-cheek reference to another man who really did find success in the fishing business, by creating fishing lures, highly collectible to this day.

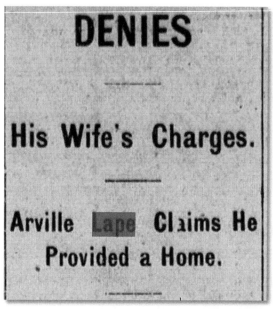

Arville Lape, whose wife, Mattie, recently instituted divorce proceedings against him, has filed an answer in which he alleges that the plaintiff is not entitled to legal separation.

He denies the charges of adultery and habitual drunkenness. The defendant claims that he had prepard a comfortable home and asked his wife to return to him. Lape asks for the care, support and custody of their two-year-old child, Cleo. At present he claims the child is living with strangers.

Akron Daily Democrat – Aug. 11, 1900 [113]

Arville's answer to Mattie's lawsuit had the look and feel of Lizzie's lawyers, Skiles, Skiles & Green. Lizzie probably hired her litigation team to help Arville.

The "strangers" that Cleo was living with, were his great-aunt and uncle, the Underwoods, well known by everyone in Lizzie's family. It is possible that when Arville said in the papers that, "he had prepared a comfortable home and asked his wife to return to him", he was angling for public support. However, it strikes one that Lizzie's family had lived so long in the glare of public attention that their private lives didn't really exist. The newspapers were there, every step of the way. There was no corn crib in which to hide.

> **Granted a Divorce.**
>
> Judge Kohler granted a divorce, Friday, to the plaintiff in the case of Mattie Lape vs. Arville Lape on the charge of habitual drunkenness. The mother was given the custody of the minor child.

Akron Beacon Journal – Dec. 7, 1900 [114]

At the end of the year, Arville lost his battle to keep his family intact. His reputation, not his mother's, was in tatters. The newspapers had made their mint of money.

By the age of 22, Arville had probably received rough treatment and training at the hands of many stepfathers, and was likely neglected by Lizzie, particularly in his early years growing up in saloons, bordellos, pool halls, and bowling alleys. Sometimes one parent's bad example is offset by the other long-suffering parent, but in his life, Arville was dealt nothing but deuces. Lizzie was so strong she rolled right over all of the men in her life and Arville was no exception.

CHAPTER 39

A Spasmodic Wave of Reform

The White Pigeon, Arville's inheritance, came with many strings attached, not least of which were the debts we learned about during our visit to the Marion County Courthouse. Until Arville reached adulthood, there were limits to the pressure his creditors could apply. But after age 21, the gloves came off. The creditors could demand their pound of flesh, and it appears they did.

Not to say Arville was an angel. He was a kid running a saloon that was rougher than he was, and he showed little interest in the job. He had a drinking problem, and was unfaithful to his young wife. After the divorce from Mattie, everyone knew all of this, via newspaper accounts.

West Church Street – Home of the White Pigeon and Lizzie

Lizzie's life in 1901 didn't hold many aces, either. In January, she lost the suit over Cliff House, and the property was sold at auction. Also in January, Lizzie was taken sick and was mentioned as "home in bed" at West Church St. This is one year after her purchase of the Jacob Lewis House. Presumably, she was back in Marion helping Arville run the Pigeon. Lizzie leased the bordello of the White Pigeon to a Madam Bunch, when another police raid occurred. The Mayor of Marion, W. H. McClure, aiming for the element of surprise, decided to raid five difference houses on the same night. Marion's men in blue snagged many birds of a feather that night – gambling houses and red light district houses, including the Pigeon, where it was reported that an officer of the peace was himself arrested. The *Star's* byline – *"A spasmodic wave of reform was in the air"*, captured the evening's successful events. Both the clients and the houses were fined. More and more, the clients themselves were being made to pay for the privilege of playing at the Pigeon, and negative publicity was accelerating for Lizzie and her family.

The newspaper coverage was relentless. The White Pigeon had gained a disreputable name for itself and anyone attached to it became newspaper fodder. Even Lizzie's daughter's accident was reported by the *Star*:

> "Mary, the little daughter of Mrs. Veon of West Church Street, stepped on a rake this morning. The teeth penetrated her right foot for quite a distance, making an ugly wound."

Marion Daily Star – August 3, 1901 [115]

Two weeks later, the *Mansfield News* picked up an article in the *Shelby Times:* a drunken bartender misnamed Orville instead of Arville, was out of control at the White Pigeon:

> Col., Aug. 11.—Orville Lape was stabbed in the thigh in a drunken row at the "White Pigeon."

Mansfield News [under Shelby Times section] – August 11, 1901 [116]

This scandalous little clipping helped sell not just one, but two newspapers. Arville's 23rd birthday was a day later on August 17th. He was still in his youth, yet his every action was constantly on public display because of his relation to Lizzie and her vice-related businesses. On September 2, 1901, the *Marion Daily Star* reported another police raid on the White Pigeon. Business as usual – with White Pigeon guests "raked into the police drag-net". The "pigeons" were not named, and the police seized guests' horses and bicycles until the fines were paid.

Officer Masterson conducted a raid at the White Pigeon after receiving a tip that there were "doings" at the White Pigeon. 1902 Marion Police Department souvenir booklet [117]

The October 10, 1901, edition of the *Marion Daily Star* reported that a renter at the White Pigeon had sued Elizabeth Veon for failure to allow access. The renter claimed she rented the place from Lizzie for $55/month. Lizzie claimed otherwise. This was yet another titillating story for the newspaper public. H. Edmund Hill, attorney for Mattie Weatherholt, the would-be renter madam, lost her case against Lizzie, but he would prove a worthy challenger later. The next newspaper story was anything but business as usual.

> "Ormel Lape, a boy about eighteen years of age [he was actually 23 years old], was arrested on suspicion Friday night by local officers. The arrest took place in the North end and the boy was taken to the city prison and locked up. He had in his possession eight pieces of railroad brass weighing about sixty-five pounds. The brass comprised car journals and other fixtures. No burglary has been reported at the police station, but the officers will investigate the matter before releasing the boy.
>
> The stolen brass was identified this morning by the officials of the Big Four Railroad, who took possession of the material. The brass had been stored in a shanty near the Junction. The door was fastened with a padlock. This was unlocked by the thief, who happened to have a key.
>
> The Lape boy had a bicycle when found by Officers Masterson and Patterson and Monahan. At first he denied being its owner, but later said that the machine belonged to him. The wheel was taken to the city prison to await investigation.
>
> Lape appeared before the mayor this afternoon, waived examination and was bound over to the grand jury in the sum of $100. He failed to give bond and is now an inmate of the county jail."

"Ormel" [Arville] Lape – "the Bicycle Bandit Boy"
Marion Daily Star, November 9, 1901 [118]

Officer Masterson was again in charge of the arrest. The 1902 souvenir police department booklet described him as "one of the oldest and best-known police officers in North Central Ohio". Obviously, he'd cut Arville and, in turn, Lizzie some slack on earlier transgressions.

This was Lizzie's worst nightmare – Arville arrested for stealing eight pieces of brass in a burglary. He was mistaken for a boy of 18 when he was in fact the 23-

year old owner of a saloon in Marion. He had a key to the shanty that he burglarized. His get-away transportation was a bicycle. His debts were piling up and he had no other business on the side like the White Pigeon's bordello house, still owned by Lizzie. He was an inept and drunken bartender whose divorced wife had remarried just 10 days earlier. Did Lizzie put him up to the theft? She had been involved in similar thefts in Lima and possibly Wapakoneta, 20 years earlier, which may have helped her purchase the White Pigeon.

CHAPTER 40

The Light at the End of the Tunnel is Another Train

Between November 1901 and the end of January 1902, Arville was held in the Marion County Jail. His stay there could not have been pleasant. The county jails were overcrowded and underfunded. The prisoner mix was indiscriminate, with hardened criminals mixed with those accused of minor offenses.

The November 6, 1902 edition headliner immediately beneath the column *"The Daily Star., By W. G. Harding.":*

> **"ARVILLE LAPE PLEADS GUILTY TO BURGLARY"** [119]

After he pled guilty to burglary of the railroad brass, justice was swift – he was processed through the courts and was lucky to land at the Mansfield Ohio Reformatory, and not sent to the Ohio State Penitentiary, a much more severe institution.

> "Girard Adams of the Mansfield Reformatory took Orville Lape to that institution today to serve an indefinite sentence."

Marion Daily Star – February 19, 1902 [120]

Upon his arrival at prison, Arville was photographed, measured, and weighed, his scars and tattoos chronicled, using the Bertillon system, known then as "Anthropometry". Under this system literally every visible bone in the body was measured, categorized and observed for unique characteristics. The method was eventually supplanted by fingerprinting. Arville himself supplied simple answers to the questions he was asked:

- Education: High School
- Religion: Episcopalian
- Known or Admitted Former Imprisonment: Lancaster
- Occupation: Bartender
- Descent: German
- Character and Habits
  - Drinks Intoxicating Liquors: yes
  - Profane: yes
  - Chew or Smoke Tobacco: yes
- Associations: Bad

On a secondary questionnaire, Arville indicated that this was his "first arrest", and yet there on the form, he stated that he had been imprisoned at some time prior in Lancaster. There might be a possible explanation for this discrepancy. The Boys' Industrial School, better known as the B.I.S., was a well-known place of imprisonment in Lancaster, Ohio, for juvenile delinquents. Of note, Lorenzo Dow Watters grew up in Lancaster. And, if Arville did spend time at the B.I.S., he would have been followed by one Leslie T. Hope *aka* Bob Hope, a young British émigré who got himself into a spot of trouble on the streets of Cleveland, Ohio. Later, Hope would make significant contributions to the B.I.S., citing the school for helping him lead a more productive and honorable life.

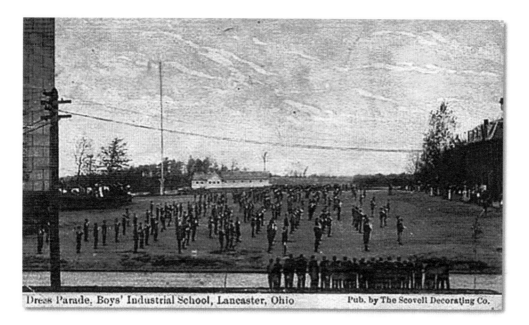

Dress Parade, Boys' Industrial School, Lancaster, Ohio.   Pub. by The Scovell Decorating Co.

Arville arrived at the Ohio State Reformatory in Mansfield in February, 1902. The facility had been proposed as early as 1868, but it took another 16 years before funding was obtained and plans secured. According to the 1803 constitution of the state of Ohio: *"...The true design of all punishment ... [was] to reform and not to exterminate mankind."* In contrast, the Ohio Penitentiary, located in Columbus, held little promise of reformation – it was merely a holding ground for hardened criminals. The hope was that younger men could be taught a trade and redeemed from a life of crime through honest enterprise and skills training. In June 1885, construction was advanced by a civic-minded group. The chosen architect of the institution was no less than Levi T. Scofield, who designed Cleveland's Civil War "Soldiers and Sailors Monument", as well as many other civic buildings of the era. In September of 1896, the institution opened to the first 150 youthful prisoners transferred from the Ohio Penitentiary in Columbus. The prisoners cheered as they arrived by train at the grand Romanesque Revival entrance of the Reformatory. It was designed to thrill and impress all of those who were lucky to be offered a second chance.

From the front, the Mansfield Reformatory looked like a palace.

From the back, it looked like what it was – a prison colony that was virtually self-sustaining.

The inmates cleaned and maintained their own facilities, grew their own food, traded products for goods needed and learned new trade skills. They worked in sales and printing offices, manned furniture, clothing, shoe, and machine factories, as well as a power plant, and a fully operational hospital, along with a chapel for worship of all denominations.[121]

If any of its stony facade looks familiar, it should, for it is where *The Shawshank Redemption* was filmed.

Which cell held Prisoner #1236?

When Arville arrived, the prison was just six years old. It was a hard life – bone-chilling in winter in the unheated cells, reeking of sweat in the summer. But the real nightmare was sharing the space with youthful criminals who were beyond reform. You could learn an honest trade, or you could become one of them and perhaps never leave the prison system at all.

The Visitor's Room was on the second floor at the very apex of the building between prison wings. It was a room filled with long tables where prisoners met visiting family members once a month, that is, if a family member felt so inclined. The guard-room, secured by iron bars running over two stories high, looked like a gorilla cage at the zoo. A family member could come and spend the entire day with the inmate, but each visitor was body searched before and after the visit. The room is beautifully restored now, but in that time, the odor of unwashed bodies was extreme, and only the hardiest of guests stayed all day.

Who visited Arville here? Certainly not his ex-wife who had remarried. Nor would she have exposed Arville's four-year old son. Arville's own father was dead. His guardian Lorenzo Dow Watters was too. His half-sister Mary was just a child of seven. No, the only likely family member who would have visited Arville, was Lizzie. She'd been imprisoned herself a few times, and understood the perils.

Declined to Pay Fire Insurance, Claiming That Liquor Was Kept In the House.

The case of Mr. Lizzie ▆▆ vs. the British Merchant Insurance Co., which has been pending in Common Pleas Court for some time, was on Friday marked settled at plaintiff's cost, without record. The contention was over a fire insurance policy. Mrs. ▆▆ conducted a hotel, known as the "Kidney House," in ▆▆ township. The building was insured, it is said, upon condition that no liquor be kept in it. Not long after the policy was obtained the building burned down, but the insurance company declined to pay the policy, claiming that it had been discovered that liquor had been kept in the house. Mrs. ▆▆ denied this and brought suit to obtain payment of the policy. In the settlement she received almost the full amount of the policy, but was obliged to pay the costs.

Akron Daily Democrat – Feb. 1, 1902 [122]

Just days before Arville was sentenced, Lizzie learned that after much litigation the insurance company would belatedly pay the policy value on the Stow fire. If the insurance money had been more forthcoming, Lizzie might have been able to help Arville pay off the White Pigeon debts. Lizzie's version of Justice didn't show up on time.

Prisoner 1236 – my great-grandfather Arville[123]

CHAPTER 41

Saving Those West-Enders

Marion Daily Star ad for West End Grain Elevator business [124] *– a sly reference to Lizzie's busy business at the nearby White Pigeon?*

A year in the life of Lizzie was always a rollercoaster ride of dreams and schemes. She filled up every one of them with conning, coaxing, and cunning, and more than enough living and loving in all of its colorful seasons. 1902 was a disaster, but only in hindsight. 1903 had prospects. She could and would make things better. Determination – she had that in spades.

There was clearly a new wind blowing in Marion. Things were not going to be the same around the White Pigeon. Arville's arrest and incarceration showed a tightening of the standards. The authorities had been trying to instill ethics in Lizzie's boomtowns for many years without much success, but with lots of kickbacks. It took the church ladies to get the job done. And it all happened in Marion in 1903.

Entrepreneur Edward Huber was determined to make a difference in Marion's wild west end. The east side had long been considered the best side of Marion, boasting fine churches and beautiful residential neighborhoods. It was *the* place to live in Marion. On the other side of town, the trains with their infernal noise, sooty environment, coal-fired odor, and dangerous crossings peppered the western edge where Lizzie's White Pigeon roosted. Long a cozy corner for low income saloons, taverns, cheap boarding houses and other types of "houses" – the west side was also the convenient and economical home for the Huber Manufacturing Company workers, too. Huber wanted more for his employees.

> **"Sour Grapes"**
>
> The following was handed us for publication by an East Marion enthusiast:
>
> "Let West Marion have the dirty factories and smoky end works and East Marion will keep its part of town nice and clean for residents and literary institutions."
>
> *Marion Daily Star – May 12, 1887* [125]

Prior to 1897 there were no churches on the west side of town. But that year, a Methodist mission was formed there, in one room of the Leader Building, with regular meetings and Sunday school for the children. The mission took firm root and Edward Huber saw a way to help his west side employees. He donated land at W. Center St. and Olney Ave., and helped raise the funds to construct a new church for the new Wesley Methodist Episcopal [M.E.] Church parish. Other business leaders joined Huber. One such civic leader was Amos H. Kling, Florence Kling DeWolfe Harding's father.

The beautiful cottage style church was completed in 1901, and opened its doors to its congregation that spring. The new church was located just one block from the White Pigeon, casting its shadow over the old coop.

*Image Courtesy of the Wesley M.E. Church History
(c/o Prospect St. United Methodist Church, Marion, Ohio)*[126]

What happened next can only be described as a miracle in Marion's western wilds. Week after week, month after month, year after year, the Wesley M.E. Church would hold evangelistic revival meetings to offer redemption to lost souls. It was a mighty appealing offer to a great many west enders. The Ladies Aid Society would be there with free refreshments, box lunches, and church socials. The Wesley Home Missions Society met in members' parlors, working to help others and spread the good word. By 1903, the religious fervor was tangible everywhere on the west side of Marion, and in other parishes, too, but the Wesley church drew the biggest crowds. Crowds so large, many worshipers had to be turned away. With heavenly voices singing beautiful songs of redemption and hope, the west side had become a joyful place.

> **IT GOES OUT OF HUMAN CONTROL**
>
> WONDERFUL MEETING AT WESLEY CHURCH
>
> **A Regular Old-Time Revival Such as Has Not Been Witnessed in Marion for Years – People Are Turned Away at Church.**
>
> "...Sunday was the greatest day Wesley Church ever saw...", "...The morning service was a time of consecration and intense religious fervor...", "...After the sermon, the alter was filled with earnest seekers and then the meeting broke out of human control. Such a scene was never witnessed, even by many who are familiar with old-time revivals..."

Marion Daily Star – Jan. 26, 1903 [127]

With so many west enders getting saved, there were very few unsaved customers left for Lizzie. Everyone was getting converted! As far as Lizzie was concerned she had just one choice:

If you can't beat them –
        – run away and get married again.

CHAPTER 42

Save Yourself or Be Damned

On February 16, 1903, Lizzie married a foreman of one of Marion's mills named William Burtelette Shetler from Shelby. She probably knew him in Shelby as well as Marion. He was a divorced father of three living children; the oldest was ten years of age. He himself was 29. Lizzie was 49.

The couple married and honeymooned in Covington, Kentucky, a perfect locale for a Kentucky madam and her newest husband. It must have reminded Lizzie of her earlier plans for an empire of adult entertainment with her husband Jack DeWitt. Covington, Kentucky, was a thriving vice-tropolis that went viral during the Civil War. Soldiers on leave from camp would cross the Ohio River and enter Kentucky where laws were loose and so were the women. Gambling, mob activity, bootlegging, and prostitution were big business. Rumor had it that the plan for Las Vegas was modeled upon Covington, Kentucky's successful empire of vice.

Lizzie was ready to be happy again. She had plans for a golden future. She was doing exactly what Lizzie did when the chips were down. But none of this answers the question of why Bill married Lizzie. Of course, he wouldn't have been the first younger man to take that step. Harry DeWitt was 11 years her junior. But 20 years! She either had what Mae West had, or perhaps he found her "considerable property" to be quite alluring. The general public thought her to be a woman of means, regardless of the facts... which may explain Bill Shetler's limited vantage point.

What happened in Covington, stayed in Covington. Did she intend to move away from Marion forever? Or did something happen there that made her change her mind? She was leaving a difficult past behind, but maybe, just maybe; she couldn't abandon Arville this time.

This was a pivotal moment in her life when she made her decision to get out of the business. She may have used her trip to Covington as a swan song to visit old friends, talk about business options in Kentucky versus Ohio; generally to assess her situation and see if and where she fit in the bigger organized market. Perhaps a moment of common sense invaded Lizzie's dreams, and she realized she was but small potatoes in the shadow of a burgeoning empire – one that was not controllable by her. She may not have been a realist, but she was an independent business woman, and nothing about the mob control in Covington would have appealed to her – unless of course she had very good friends at the top. In Marion, she was a big fish in a little pond; in Covington, she was a nobody. She'd had more than her fill of that in Stow.

Like it or not, Lizzie was getting older. Her line of woman's work, may originally have seemed exotic, erotic and freeing; but at age 49, she along with the general public, must have begun to recognize it for what it was – tawdry, seamy and enslaving. And the competition was younger.

In recent years, Lizzie had grown closer to her son whom she'd probably left behind in Plain City with his father when she had decided to restart her life of crime and vice. It was only after young Arville was foisted on her by the court system that she had to develop some makeshift parenting skills. If she moved to Covington, she could not help him. And he did need her help now. Why she did what she did was not written up in the *Marion Daily Star*, unlike most everything else in her life.

Pike Street – Covington, Kentucky

CHAPTER 43

Repent and Give Interviews

On August 1, 1903, Arville was paroled from the Ohio Reformatory in Mansfield. He was 25 years old, and had served just over one year behind prison bars. Before he was released from jail, Arville secured a job at the Marion Malleable Iron Works. John A. Huber, corporate secretary, signed Arville's work papers. John was the nephew of Edward Huber, the industrialist who donated the land for and built the Wesley M.E. Church. Edward Huber was also the founder of the Malleable Iron works. If your family was in Ohio farming in the early 1900's, you knew what a "Huber" threshing machine was, because your family either owned or hired one of those steam-powered big-bellied cylindrical tractors at harvest time.

Steam Engine Threshing in Central Ohio [128]

The Huber family kept everybody employed in Marion, and made it the boomtown it truly was in Lizzie's and Arville's time. It was important for paroled men to have jobs when they left the reformatory. Otherwise, they were more likely to return to crime and next time, if they were old enough, it might mean a trip to the Ohio Penitentiary in Columbus. Of the parolees who were released around the time Arville was paroled, several of them violated their paroles and were returned to prison.

By the time Arville was fully discharged from his prison term on July 29, 1904, he had switched jobs and cities and was working at the Shelby Tube Works in Shelby. A lot of things could happen in a year, and did.

Shelby Tube Steel Workers, 1902, Annealing Night Gang. Courtesy The Shelby Museum of History, Shelby, Ohio.[129] *Upper left looks like Arville Lape*

(Note – Google Facial Recognition Software matched this photo to Arville's)

In September of 1903, Mattie – Arville's ex-wife and my great-grandmother – filed for divorce from her second husband Robert E. Burns. It was a disastrous second marriage on the heels of her divorce from Arville in 1900. Mattie was working as a maid when Arville was paroled in August of 1903. In November of 1903, the judge granted Mattie a divorce from her abusive husband of two years. Two weeks later, Mattie and Arville remarried in Shelby. Once released, Arville made a lot of things happen in short order. He had had plenty of time to think things through in jail and a chance to dry out and learn a machinist trade.

Barberton Pottery Co. / A. J. Cartright Supt. Barberton Ohio		Discharged July 29, 1904
C. C. Mitchell Livoy Ohio		Violated parole Dec 8, 1903. Imprisoned in the Colorado Penitentiary instead of Reformatory in Ohio
L.J.R. Co. E. W. McCoslin Asst. Supt. #31 Franklin St Akron Ohio		Discharged July 29, 1904
M. C. Keller Shelby Ohio		Discharged July 25, 1904
Geo. W. Amos #1003 East Hoffman Ave. Dayton Ohio		Discharged Aug 17/04
Norton Bros. #38 Genova St Cleveland Ohio		Violated parole & is wanted. Returned Nov. 23 – 1905. Certificate of Release 1/21/15
The Marion Mall Iron Co. Jno. A. Huber Supt. Marion Ohio / Shelby Fusaka Shelby O.		Discharged July 29, 1904
V. J. Fagin M.S. Marshal Cincinnati Ohio		Violated RELEASED MAR 29 19 Nov 23rd 1905

Ohio Reformatory of Mansfield Ohio – Release Record (2nd from last)[130]

That must have helped him focus on what was important. He needed to stay out of trouble when he left that place. He managed to leave the reformatory in one piece, maintain his parole, and never return.[131] That was a feat. Lorenzo Dow Watters would have been proud.

Cleo and Mattie – reunited with Arville after his release[132]

Yet can we credit all of Arville's good fortune in landing a solid job with a wealthy sponsor to his own abilities or to Lorenzo's training? Was this the way Lizzie's world worked? Not likely, nor does it still. You needed to have connections. You needed people on your side. You needed to have friends in a friendless town. You needed to join them. You needed good PR.

Lizzie had returned from Covington, Kentucky to Marion, ahead of Arville's parole and she had a plan, putting it into action less than two weeks after she married Bill Shetler. Lizzie came home to Marion *and* Shelby. The ever-present newspapers were there to catch the action.

LIZZIE VEON IS CONVERTED

Mayor Long, of Shelby, does not pose as a revivalist but at the same time he is the sort of a fellow who always has a good word for everybody. Many a man and woman who has disobeyed the law and come before him for trial has been given some good advice. It is not every chief executive who would interest himself enough to give advice to the offenders who come before him for transgressing the law yet Mayor Long has made a practice of speaking a kind word to the unfortunate men and owmen who have been the victims of police court. No one can tell how much good he has done in this manner but it is the object of the Globe today to cite only one incident in this connection. It may seem almost impossible to credit the story but when the facts are given in a letter and signed by the person undergoing the change of heart one cannot help but believe.

The story reads like a romance. Mrs. Lizzie Veon came to Shelby over two years ago and started a house of ill repute near the junction, the resort being known as the "White Pigeon." spoke those touching words to me. How often I have wished for those touching words again. They touched my heart as it was never touched before but thank the Lord it has been touched with the Spirit. That has been over two years and I am certain I have been under conviction ever since. but thank God I have now found peace in Christ Jesus. No one knows what one kind word will do. If I remember correctly I could not look you in the face but now I thank God I can look the world in the face and say I will serve God all the rest of my days.

There was a lady running a house of ill repute here and I prayed for God to touch her heart with some sort of a feeling that she might leave the place in peace. She had a lease for two years but she left before her months were up.

The first thing God asked me to do was to go to a saloon and pray for the owner and I went cheerfully and will go just as often as God wants me to. There is nothing will close up saloons but the kindness of God's people and the power he gives them to talk and pray. These words you spoke to me in

both columns continued on next page...

It was under the strict surveillance of the police and not many weeks elapsed before Mrs. Veon, as proprietress, was ordered to appear before Mayor Long on the charge of conducting a house of ill fame. She denied the charge but Mayor Long had the word of the police that she was guilty and he so informed her. After assessing a fine which was paid he talked to her kindly about the business she was engaged in. He reminded her of the fact that she was passed middle age and that she would not want to be in that sort of business all her life. She had a daughter ten years of age and the mayor reminded her of the influence the mother's life would have upon the child. All the facts were brought forcibly home to her and she cried like a child. Notwithstanding this she continued in the business finally selling out and leaving the city, going to Marion her former home, where she engaged in the same business. Before leaving Shelby she married William Shetler. The following letter was received by Mayor Long which fully explains the foundation for this story:

    Marion, O., March 2, 1904.
Mayor Long, Shelby, Ohio.

 Dear Sir—I know you will be greatly surprised to receive a letter from such a poor sinner as I was when you kindness have haunted me ever since and I have just begun to realize where I stood and now I pray that God may give you the spirit to touch some one else's heart as you did mine with kind words. All of our little ones are good little Christians.

 You can do as you please with this letter. Have it printed in the Globe if you like for I am not ashamed for the world to know that I and my children belong to God. Now if you feel as if you ought to answer this letter alright or I should be pleased to receive a letter from your wife.

 There has been a great deal of guessing as to Mr. Shetler and I being married. I desire to say that we are married but we were not married in the state of Ohio. The people may take your money but thank God they can't take the Holy Ghost out of your hearts. What God gives you no one can take away. I was once Mrs. Veon but now Mrs. Shetler, 430 West Church street, Marion, Ohio.

 In closing I want to thank you very much for the kind words you spoke to me, you may never know how much good you have done by that kindly talk you gave me.

    Very respectfully,
    MRS. LIZZIE SHETLER.
    —Shelby Globe.

Mansfield Daily Shield – March 6, 1903 from The Shelby Globe – March 2, 1903 [133]

 This is the rarest of rare documents – a first person account by Lizzie herself. I'd written her narrative, thought I had the whole of it, and then discovered this document via Google News Archive online service. Outrageous – to have her edit my manuscript from the grave. (Another act of serendipity to delight in, after nearly forty years of looking.)

 So what can we deduce from this open letter to the Mayor of Shelby, Ohio?

Here were the high points:

- Lizzie Veon was converted.
- Lizzie confessed openly to her sins.
- It was revealed here that her house in Shelby and her house in Marion *both* were known as the White Pigeon!
- Lizzie called upon the public to protect the children (think *her* children).
- Lizzie told doubters that she was married out of state to Bill Shetler.
- She prayed for others like her and visited saloons to spread the news.

From this very public platform which had frequently been used against her, Lizzie turned the tables giving it a positive spin, and in the process created a great deal of good will. She didn't just stop in Shelby. She went on to Marion and gave this interview:

> Marion – Mrs. Lizzie Shettler, as a result of the wave of reform which has swept over this city, as an aftermath of the big revivals here, has tendered the use of the building known as "The White Pigeon", and the saloon on the same premises, to the Wesley M. E. Church, the former to be used as a mission and the latter as a coffee house. Mrs. Shettler says the premises shall never again be used for immoral purposes and that, should she sell the place, a part of the proceeds will be given to the church."

Marion Daily Star – March 17, 1903 [134]

What a perfect solution, volunteer the tainted Pigeon to the revivalist church. Make it a mission for unwed mothers. There is sweet justice in this for one and all. As a savvy businesswoman, Lizzie was offering up a win-win opportunity to the community.

Between March and August 1903, the local papers were silent about Lizzie. This could mean that she was indeed out of the "house" business. Then, in August, just four days after Arville is paroled, the *Marion Daily Star – August 5, 1903* [135] revealed exactly where Mrs. Shetler had been during those intervening months.

"Work in the South" – Women's Home Mission Society of the Wesley M.E. Southern-born Mrs. Shetler is reporting mission work for the Bureau of Texas:

> **Wesley Missionary Program.**
>
> The W. H. M. [Women's Home Mission] society of Wesley M. E. Church will meet at the home of Mrs. Charles Winfield of Wood Street, Thursday, at 2:30 p.m., subject, "Work in the South."
>
> The following is the program to be rendered:
>
> Singing, "Help Us, O Lord", No. 904.
>
> Scripture lesson, Cor. 2-9, Mrs. Elliot.
>
> Prayer, Mrs. Wideman.
>
> Bureau of Georgia, Miss Carter.
>
> Music, Cleo Cloud.
>
> Bureau of Florida, Miss Ash.
>
> Bureau for Texas, <u>Mrs. Shettler</u>. [Lizzie]
>
> Home and schools in the South, Mrs. Luellen.
>
> Recitation, Bertha Eaton.
>
> Business.
>
> Social hour.
>
> Refreshments.
>
> Everyone is invited.

This old sinner knew the value of positive PR when she created it. Misters John and Edward Huber helped Lizzie help her son. She helped rebuild a neighborhood by leaving it. Lizzie saved her son by being saved.

Chapter 44

The Feathered Noose is Loose

In 1904 The White Pigeon was sold. Lizzie had found a buyer. A farmer's family named Weir bought the Pigeon for $5,500. Lizzie was free – Arville and Mattie too – of a way of life that had become obsolete. All three of their names plus Bill Shetler's – were on the deed of sale.

Perhaps Lizzie met the Weir family at one of the M.E. Church socials. Then again, it is possible that the Weir family thought they too, could make a mint of money on the White Pigeon, because on March 17, 1906, the police were back in business raiding the place and collecting madams and inmates! The White Pigeon had risen again like a Phoenix from the ashes.

> **POLICE RAID TWO RESORTS**
>
> Chief and Captain Make Several Arrests.
>
> **NO PATRONS ARE CAUGHT IN THE RAID**
>
> "...Chief Cornwell and Captain Patterson, between the hours of 8 and 9 o'clock, Friday evening, raided the resorts of Carrie Heilman, who conducted the place formerly owned by George Greeno; and Margaret Kenzie, who runs what is commonly known as the "White Pigeon."

Marion Daily Star – March 17, 1906 [136]

The White Pigeon was resurrected and flying again. No mention of the Weir family. It seems they sold or leased it to one of the ladies mentioned in the raid.

> **POLICE RAID A WEST END HOUSE**
>
> Inmates of White Pigeon Are Taken Before Mayor.
>
> **PATRONS OF HOUSE ARE ALSO ARRESTED**
>
> Fines Are Paid This Morning – Raid Is Made Because Edith Glenn Is Being Sheltered in the Resort in Secrecy – A Few Notes from the Police Court.
> One of the West End resorts known as the White Pigeon was raided by the police at 11:20 o'clock Thursday evening and the arrest of ten persons followed. Edith Glenn, better known as "Cinnamon Brown", was the cause of the raid. The woman had been ordered to stay away from the city and the police learning that she was being sheltered at the White Pigeon, decided to pull the place.

Marion Daily Star – June 15, 1906 [137]

This was the final mention in print of the White Pigeon – It was no longer used as a mission for unwed mothers, if it ever was.

Meanwhile, romance was waning for the newlyweds – both generations – first Lizzie and Bill, then Mattie and Arville.

> Hearing on motion for alimony pending suit in the divorce case of Elizabeth Shetler vs. Wm. Shetler was set for this morning in probate court and quite a large number of witnesses and spectators were in attendance. Skiles, Green & Skiles of Shelby, are the attorneys for the plaintiff, and DeGolley & DeGolley, of Marion, and J. P. Seward for the defendant. Plaintiff asked for divorce, alimony and injunction, alleging gross neglect of duty on the part of defendant, who in his cross petition came back with certain sensational allegations relative to plaintiff's conduct while in Marion. Claiming that she had abundant property the defendant asked for alimony from her and eleven affidavits were filed in the case. A conference was held at which the matter of alimony was settled between the parties and the hearing on the divorce petition was continued.

"Certain Sensational Allegations" – Mansfield News, Sept. 9, 1905 [138]

> In the probate court case of Elizabeth Shetler vs. Wm. Shetler plaintiff has been granted a divorce on the ground of defendant's gross neglect of duty. Her property is restored to her, her husband being divested of any interest in it. It is ordered that defendant pay her $200 alimony.

Mansfield Daily Shield, Oct. 30, 1905 [139]

As with so many of her court cases, Lizzie won. The trial might have been sensational and the courtroom packed with spectators, but Lizzie prevailed again, keeping her property *and* also collecting alimony from young William. Her lawyers once again, earned their fees. This was a woman blazing trails in a court system where less than a generation earlier, married women were divested of their property as part of the marriage bond. This was a whole new form of progressive justice, and it took gutsy women like Lizzie to push the door wide open.

And from the *Akron Beacon Journal, January 22, 1906:* [140]

> **Seeks a Divorce**
>
> *"Sheriff Barker on Monday served a copy of a petition for divorce upon Mattie Lape of Cuyahoga Falls, who has been sued by her husband, Henry Lape, in Richland County. The husband seeks a divorce on the grounds of extreme cruelty."*

Here's a twist. Arville sued Mattie for cruelty and is asking her for a divorce. Not the other way around? And Mattie had obviously moved back to Cuyahoga Falls, her home with the Underwoods by that time.

> **Divorce Granted.**
>
> A divorce has been granted in probate court to Henry A. Lape from Mattie A. Lape on the ground of defendant's extreme cruelty. Plaintiff is awarded the custody of the child.

Mansfield Daily Shield, Mar. 17, 1906 [141]

As improbable as it sounds, ex-con Arville gained custody of his son Cleo. What could have caused a judge to turn over a child of eight years to Arville and in turn, Lizzie? What cruelty could a wife inflict on a husband that would be grounds for such an unusual decision? There are only these two newspaper accounts, and they are mute.

One key point not reported here is whether or not Mattie fought for custody at all. A few observations: never again was Arville arrested for drinking, carousing, or stealing, and in all ways outwardly, he appeared reformed. He worked hard and earned an honest living. The one incident that was relayed by Cleo about his father, indicated that Arville maintained a zero tolerance for certain vices, in this case, smoking tobacco. When Cleo as a boy was discovered smoking corn silk behind the barn, Arville told him, "If I ever catch you smoking again, I'll shoot it out of your mouth." Spoken like a man with a mission to keep his son free from his own demons. And one who was handy with a gun. Where others might have inherited a sunny disposition, Cleo inherited Arville's Iver Johnson 7-shot 22 caliber pistol. The sunny disposition must have been from his mother's side of the family.

We do not know for sure what could have driven Mattie away. However, learning a little bit more about her, long after Arville, I suspect she developed an intolerance for vice of any kind. Much later in her life, Mattie took in one or two roomers at a time at her home for the additional income. Keeping "roomers" who rented a bedroom and had access to her kitchen, meant that certain house rules had to be observed – no late nights, no drinking, and no guests. When a roomer broke a rule, they were warned, and if they ignored the warning, they were evicted. That was that. I suspect that Arville broke one or more of her "house" rules for husbands. Her response was to go home to her mother's family. I understand now what made her tough enough to fire bad renters. She was a gutsy woman, too. Who knew that when we were watching great-grandma Mattie in action with her boarding house business that we were in fact meeting the ghost of Lizzie, ruling her house with an iron hand?

Chapter 45

Hard-Headed Romantics

My reformed family may have learned their legal lessons well, but they were eternally the marrying kind. Romance was again in the air in 1907 for Arville and Mattie… this time not for each other. Mattie chose a stage hand from Akron, and Arville fell for a girl, well…. Not to say, his love interest, Lottie Coulter was "in the business", but she was up to her pretty ears in husbands, ex-husbands, and bigamist-husbands in jail and on the lam. She must have been the "marrying kind", too. All told, Lottie Coulter married seven times. Arville met his match with this wife number four, apparently. Based on the following newspaper account, Arville may have married at least one other woman. She remains to this day, unknown and at large.

GOES TO ALTAR FOR FOURTH TIME

Shelby Woman Becomes Wife of a Man from Missouri

HER EX-HUSBANDS ARE ALL LIVING

One of Them is Serving Time Out in the Reformatory

There was a great rush of business in the courts of Squires Schaeffer and Jarvis Wednesday afternoon. Squire Schaeffer went to the court house with one of his customers to secure some necessary papers. They had to wait their turn. A man by the name of Henry A. Lape was securing a license to marry Lottie Coutler-Hayman-Stewart-Delancy, a much married woman of Shelby.

When Lape got his license and started out, the clerk told Squire Schaeffer that the would-be bride-groom was on the hunt of a justice. Squire Schaeffer got the papers for his client and hurried back to the office to be ready for the other party.

He was met at the foot of the stairs by his constable, who told him there was a couple in the office who wished to be made one, temporarily, at least. The obliging Squire hurried upstairs, but the anxious couple had got tired of waiting and had been "tied up" by Squire Jarvis about five minutes before

ing bride has met her fate.

Mrs. Lape's ex-husbands are all living. Her first husband, Hayman, is a well known resident of Shelby; Stewart, the second husband, is doing time for bigamy in the Mansfield reformatory, while Delancy is running at large in the vicinity of Shelby.

The prospective bridal party entered the office of Squire Jarvis. The bride waited there till the groom went into the rear office. The justice did not happen to be in, so there was some delay. The bridegroom grew impatient.

"Gee, this thing of getting married it getting to be an old story with me," he remarked carelessly. "Why, have you been married before?" asked a visitor who happened to be in the office.

The man held up four fingers significantly.

"Does she know it?" ask the visitor.

"No. What's the use of tellin' her?"

The man, lowered his voice to a confidential whisper, and this time held up three fingers, saying, "she's been married three times."

When asked if he had married the same woman each time, Lape replied. "I did that twice. But I like a change."

Justice Jarvis then arrived and made this couple one. After the ceremony, the newly wedded couple sprung a pleasant little surprise on Justice Jarvis. They told him that he had performed a similar ceremony for each of them, but to different parties.

Mansfield Daily Shield July 5, 1907 [142]

"Gee, this thing of getting married is getting to be an old story with me."

During this season of second chances, was Arville's son being raised by Lizzie?

As crazy as that sounds, it was likely. Mattie was making poor choices for herself, and barely making ends meet living with her new husband and his mother. In fact, in the 1910 census, Mattie did not even list that she had any children at all. Meanwhile, Arville, inheriting Lizzie's love of love, was busy with Lottie, a lady of odd repute. There was no one left to raise Cleo, but Lizzie.

Lizzie was mother to Mary, just two years older than Cleo, and in fact our immediate family was for many years confused about Mary's relationship to my grandfather. Was she a half sister to Cleo? Was she an aunt of Cleo's? Yet, there she was in the photos with Cleo and with Lizzie, at the same time and in the same cities of Marion and Shelby. That Cleo was being raised by Lizzie, was confirmed by the 1910 census, where he was listed as a member of Lizzie's household.

The time period of 1908-1910 was quiet. There were no news items or comedic sketches of Lizzie and the Law, or Lizzie and the Judge, or Lizzie and the White Pigeon. In 1908 she was 55 years old. When Lizzie told the newspapers in Marion that she was giving up the White Pigeon, she was a woman of her word.

The papers too, had a code of ethics. Lizzie was no longer a serial storyline. She was out of the glare of public scrutiny. Perhaps the fact that she was raising young children, helped. In the 1906 Shelby City Directory she was listed as living at "1 Earl Ave." along with Mary and Arville and presumably unlisted Cleo. After Arville's wedding, he and Lottie took rooms at the "New Shelby Inn" on Broadway & Main, according to the 1908-1909 directory, while Arville worked at the nearby Brightman Mfg. Company. This was such a quiet time in Lizzie's life in the papers, that it seemed unnatural. What was she up to? She wasn't listed in the Shelby directory in 1907. Where did she go?

Cleo Lape (b. 1898) and his Aunt Mary Veon (b. 1896)
– two generations raised by Lizzie simultaneously[143]

In my newspaper searches online, I stumbled onto a story in Newark, Ohio, dated April 24, 1905. This would have been around the time that Lizzie separated from Bill Shetler – a low point in her life, no doubt. A madam named Lizzie Rogers was a witness for the State of Ohio in a love triangle murder that centered on her house activities on Railroad Street in Newark. Another house near the railroad tracks. It must have been another Lizzie Rogers, but it was a tantalizing story. Newark's problems made Marion's and Shelby's social evils seem like child's play. Yet, there was that one tiny thread of a connection – Newark itself – which would play a part later in Lizzie's life when the stage would shift back to eastern Ohio.

In 1908 she married yet again, this time a farmer from Warren Township in

Tuscarawas County. He owned 13 acres of his father's homestead. For years I knew that Lizzie married a man named France, because the walnut box misspelled it out – "Elizebeth France". But what of this Mr. France? Fortunately, Dad remembered some names from his own childhood – Scott and Addie France and their son Randall, from a friendly family visit. That was something to go on.

However she did not marry Mr. France in Tuscarawas County. She married him in Norwalk, Ohio of Huron County. What was she doing so far north of Shelby?

Groom's Name:	**J. D. France**	Groom's Father's Name:	Michael France
Groom's Birth Date:	1849	Groom's Mother's Name:	Catharine Albaugh
Groom's Birthplace:	Newcumberland, Ohio	Bride's Father's Name:	Lewis Rogers
Groom's Age:	59	Bride's Mother's Name:	Betsy Rose
Bride's Name:	Elizabeth Veson	Groom's Marital Status:	**Divorced**
Bride's Birth Date:	1859	Bride's Marital Status:	Widowed
Bride's Birthplace:	Whitley Co, Ky	Indexing Project (Batch) Number:	M02310-5
Bride's Age:	49	System Origin:	Ohio-EASy
Marriage Date:	19 May 1908	Source Film Number:	410265
Marriage Place:	Huron, Ohio	Reference Number:	p 125 cn 426

Marriage Record for J.D. France and Elizabeth Veon [144]

Here was evidence of the two perennial romantics getting married in Huron, Ohio: home of Cedar Point, a great amusement park and home of the beautiful Breakers Hotel. Would Lizzie want to honeymoon there? But of course! Amusement was her middle name. (Technically, it was Amy.) The typo on her surname – Veson for Veon – and the unexpected location kept me from discovering this record long ago.

*J.D. France & Elizabeth Veon's Marriage Record
Huron County, Norwalk, Ohio – May 19, 1908* [145]

Interesting that she listed as her parents – Lewis and Betsy Rogers – the same as in her church marriage to Charles W. Veon. However, her birth parents' given names were Prior and Cynthia Rogers, from the 1860 census. Since she did not appear in the census until 1880 with Jeremiah and Arville, it is just possible that she was raised by this Rogers family in place of her natural parents. A relative's family perhaps? She was only seven years old in that first 1860 Whitley County census, and possibly with a little further research, more can be uncovered about Lizzie's distant Civil War period past. It was in these war years, that Lizzie developed significant survival skills. We have her word that Lewis and Betsy were her parents' names, and over time I've come to listen more carefully for the truth of her story.

In point of fact Lizzie and John D. France were married in Huron *County*, Ohio, not the *City* of Huron – home of Cedar Point. Norwalk, Ohio is the Huron County seat, a full 18 miles from the "greatest amusement park in the world". From the county court records in Norwalk, it would appear that she and J. D. made a full day of it on their wedding day of May 19, 1908. At 8:15 am that morning, she purchased a 12 acre parcel of land in Greenfield Twp., Huron County, for $800 in her name alone. Doesn't everyone begin their wedding day with a non-spousal real estate purchase?

By the end of the day, Lizzie Veon of "North Fairfield" in Huron County, was married to John D. France of New Cumberland in Tuscarawas County, by the Rev. Herbert Agate of the Norwalk Baptist Church.

*North Fairfield, Ohio – a survivor from Lizzie's day
- graphic by Miranda Peters* [146]

What attracted her to North Fairfield, a town that by 1908 was well known to have been bypassed by the railroads? This was not Lizzie's typical modus operandi. If she was still working the shady side of the street in North Fairfield, she was no longer dependent on the railroads to deliver her customers. Lizzie's traffic pattern was changing. There had been this brand-new invention by Henry Ford called the mass-production assembly line in Detroit, which made 1908 a banner year for his famed "Model T". Suddenly, the middle classes could travel in their own "Tin Lizzie" to every disreputable corner of Ohio. Lizzie's enterprising horizons broadened considerably.

Ridiculous at this late date to hope for a change of character from such a character as was Lizzie. Yet, I do. I want her to be less hard-hearted than she apparently was. For in this last known marriage record, is contained my full understanding that she was trading her ***self*** for property, as concisely as:

Step 1: Get a protector to buy you property.
Step 2: Make sure it is deeded in your name only and not your husband's.
Step 3: Get married/services rendered.

It couldn't be more plainly written. And it's right there in the progression of court records in Norwalk, Ohio. Trust wasn't in her DNA. Lizzie was always a businesswoman, first, not last.

CHAPTER 46

Down On the Farm

New Cumberland, Ohio is almost a ghost town now. It wasn't when Lizzie lived nearby on the John France farm in Warren Twp., Tuscarawas County. No, it was not until 1936 that the Atwood Reservoir was completed and the nearby town of Atwood was purchased, demolished, and flooded, that the adjacent town of New Cumberland started to dry up. When the Atwood Lake level is lowered by the Corps of Engineers, you can see the visible signs of the old rail line that now runs directly into the flooded lake bed.

If you look at New Cumberland from an aerial map, you will see that the New Cumberland Cemetery consumes roughly one quarter of the town as it exists today. Whoever said "none of us gets out of here alive" may have visited New Cumberland, no longer a village, but instead annexed to the adjacent village of Mineral City. The mineral in Mineral City was coal. Strip mines dotted Tuscarawas County. It was a hard working corner of the world in the early part of the 20th century. Now, it looks exhausted.

If Lizzie was purposefully trying to escape her past, she couldn't have run to a more remote and primitive corner of Ohio. But was she running from her past or *to* it? Because, New Cumberland, Ohio, and Warren Township in particular, look a whole lot like Whitley County, Kentucky – rolling hills, coal mining and all.

John D. France was a descendant of one of the homesteaders of Warren Twp. J. D.'s grandfather John was an early Ohio settler. J. D.'s parents and in turn, siblings inherited their 130-acre farm.

J.D. France farmed there, with his first wife Mary. They had two children living to adulthood – Scott and Catherine, Scott being the gentleman who brought his wife and son to visit Cleo and my dad's family long ago. After Mary died in 1892, J. D. married a widow named Mrs. Leggett. That marriage did not work out amicably and they divorced. Lizzie was wife number three in 1908.

How Lizzie met J. D. France is a mystery. However, there might have been a possible Stow connection. On the 1874 map of Stow, well ahead of Lizzie's arrival, a mile or so north of Cliff House, is a lot on Darrow Rd. apparently owned by a *"J. France"*. Was this Lizzie's eighth husband, John D. France? Maybe. In her saloon business, she had lots of opportunity to meet people traveling by train across the continent. He didn't have to live down the block for Lizzie to have known him well.

by Cleo Lape[147]

The 1910 census for Warren Township, Tuscarawas County, is the freeze frame photo of the family "down on the farm" listing John and Lizzie France, with Mary Veon and Cleo Lape. The same census shows Lizzie's son Arville and daughter-in-law Lottie. By 1910, they had moved to Utica, Ohio, not far from Newark, and were living in a house alongside and rented from Lottie's parents. Not a bad idea, to keep an eye on their re-marrying-kind of daughter. Arville and Lottie purchased the lot from her parents two years later. Mattie, Arville's ex-wife/Cleo's mother was living in Akron in 1910 with her husband George Merwin, a Colonial Theatre stage hand. In the census, Mattie indicated that she had no children, denying Cleo's existence.

In 1913, Mary Veon fell in love with a local boy named Floyd Huff, and a baby was born before the nine months was out. Lizzie's second grandson did not live out the year, and was buried in the New Cumberland Cemetery in an unmarked grave. Then in 1915, Virgil Huff was born to Floyd and Mary – a third grandson for Lizzie, and a first cousin for Cleo. These were happy times down on the farm in New Cumberland.

In 1916, family life on the farm and in the cities changed for everyone. Arville Lape died unexpectedly from an injury sustained while riding on the back of a friend's motorcycle. Lizzie's wild child was gone.

Arville was laid to rest in an unmarked grave in Southlawn Cemetery in Utica. His obituary in the Utica Herald was the last mention of Arville in the papers. It was also the last mention of Lizzie by the press. Although, she could not have understood my curiosity, any more than I can understand her motives, the only way I learned Lizzie's strange story at all, was through historical newspaper references. With Lizzie out of the limelight, she became as so many of our other ancestors – inscrutable except for the standard announcement of birth, marriage, and death. And in the end, she managed to avoid even that.

CHAPTER 47

Saving Lizzie

The last word on the notorious life of Lizzie ended with an obituary that was not her own. Yet there was one other narrative that could shed light on two more years of Lizzie's life – the journals of her grandson Cleo.

After Cleo's father died, it was apparent that his step-mother Lottie and his grandma Lizzie could no longer care for Cleo. Cleo would have to live with his mother Mattie in Akron. However Mattie was on the road a great deal, traveling the eastern states as a sales lady for the Larkin Soap Company. Periodically she would return to Akron and to her husband George.

On July 13, 1916, at the age of 17, just one day after his father died, Cleo wrote in his diary, "Arrived in Akron". It was clearly a new beginning for Cleo. His journals spanning 1916 through 1918 give an account of a young man about town, making the most of every adventure. Once again, he moved in with his mother's Shannon cousins – Lilly Underwood's daughter Minnie Underwood Sullivan and her young family – detailing every mile, every nickel spent and earned, every person visited, every letter written and received. It is a charming diary of simplicity and enthusiasm.

You may ask, where was Lizzie? Why she was evidently still "down on the farm", as Cleo affectionately called Lizzie and J. D. France's New Cumberland property. His diary tallied dozens of letters written and received by Cleo to and from Lizzie. Not one letter survives. But his diary mentions a wonderful Thanksgiving party hosted in New Cumberland where Cleo is feted and treated like royalty. Lizzie is evident in the diary's mention of a hand-tailored vest made by Lizzie and delivered to Cleo. Lizzie came to Akron several times to visit Cleo and reveled with him on trips to Stow's Silver Lake Amusement Park and to see live theater at Akron's Music Hall including the sentimental blockbuster "Shepherd of the Hills". Lizzie was full of support and affirmation for young Cleo.

Live theater that Lizzie and Cleo attended April 23, 1918 –with a storyline that would have appealed to her.[148]

In 1918, Cleo was 20 to Lizzie's 65. They both shared the bond of loving Arville, but not being able to save him. Lizzie had already stepped into the parental void for Cleo, years earlier. And Cleo, like all grandchildren, would have looked on Lizzie with love, tolerance, and patience for a grandparent's foibles. Lizzie was there for Cleo, every step of the way.

Simply put, Cleo was Lizzie's redemption, surely as Arville was her cross to bear.

Cleo – "newly arrived" and overlooking East Akron from the top of the Goodyear Plant[149]

CHAPTER 48

[Still] Looking For Lizzie

So what may we conclude? Should we be mortified by Lizzie's immoral behavior? She was bad. She preyed on men. She used husbands like beach towels. When things got tough, she didn't stick around. She didn't fit in anyone's code book of ethics. My family stopped talking about her completely.

Lizzie's lifestyle of offering herself up on the altar of property ownership, when thievery and trafficking in flesh proved too risky – was her self-interpretation of women's "rights". Lizzie was a woman without a childhood, who traded in flesh but never in spirit. She tried too late to become a better mother to her son, but got a second chance in becoming a loving force in my grandfather's young life – raising him when his own parents were unable to do it. She had the political will and believed in the American justice system. She invested so much of her money and energy in our American legal system, "she should have been a lawyer", as the old saloon joke goes.

But what of her other traits? Was she not an independent, entrepreneurial woman in an age of repression? Did she not demand equal rights for women in the courts and property rights, when it was unheard of? Was she engaged in the politics of the day, as few women had been? And who could not help but call her a veteran of the Civil War? Her motivations were her own, but in a twist of logic, her disreputable trail-blazing resulted in progress for *all* women.

And then there's that one Lizzie characteristic that nearly cost me my loving family, but in the end, saved it. She kept moving forward relentlessly. Sometimes leaving loved ones behind, like her son Arville, and perhaps other family members left in some sooty train station back on the track. She did not stop her forward motion, the train kept rolling. And on the hard journey, Lizzie learned from her mistakes the inevitable way, retracing old ground until she did. Lizzie's life was loaded with restarts. She married eight times, she opened and closed dozens of businesses, she lived in as many towns, she was wealthy and broke in cyclic fashion. And, she managed to raise a grandchild better than she did her own son. She was lucky to get that second chance... and so was our family.

Somehow, she'd survived the horror of the Civil War. And when the withering war ended, she drank up life and blossomed like the rugged Kentucky wildflower that she was. To the end of her days, she stayed thirsty for life.

Which brings us to the subject of what happened to Lizzie at the end of her days... no one knows.

She sailed off the map with the end of Cleo's 1918 journals. Although she was living in New Cumberland where J. D.'s farm was located, it is not known for certain that she was still married to J. D. France after 1918. It is possible that she remarried. However, we *can* trace J. D. France himself, well beyond 1918. In the 1920 census, he was listed as living with his children Scott and Addie France in New Philadelphia, the seat of Tuscarawas County; and as "widowed", not divorced. But, as we've seen in past records, he might have chosen to describe himself either way, since he was widowed by his first wife, but divorced by wife number two – ahead of Lizzie, wife number three. So little time; so many spouses.

If Lizzie died still married to J. D., perhaps she was buried with him. But if that was the case, no death certificate for this period of time fit Lizzie. No sign of an obituary, either. And, the funeral home that provided the burial services for J. D. France, had no records for Lizzie.

Lizzie's Thanksgiving party in 1917 completed her transformation from madam to matriarch. It is ironic, that her 1882 invitation to a Thanksgiving feast at the American House Hotel with B. W. Johnson, was her ticket from mother to madam. I've combed through more "Elizabeth/Lizzie France" death certificates in and around Ohio, purchasing many of them along the way, much as a gambler continues to buy lottery tickets, because *this* one could be a winner. The Ohio Historical Archives should erect a special wing in Lizzie's honor, as I have helped fund it.

When Lizzie's daughter Mary died, she was buried in the New Cumberland Cemetery, presumably alongside her infant son and her husband Floyd. Mary's unmarried son Virgil Huff, who died in 1971 before his mother, was the sole descendant of Lizzie's to have an actual grave marker in the New Cumberland Cemetery. And such a lonely corner of the cemetery it was. The most remote corner, but nearest the France farm as the crow flies. Or, a white pigeon.

So we have no final resting place for Lizzie, which is fitting, because she never rested. Did she run off and marry again? Perhaps. She was only 65 years old in

1918, and a spry 65, visiting amusement parks, music halls and movie theaters with her grandson. Too bad she didn't have a given name as unusual as her son Arville. It would have made the search easier.

Yet, even as I write this, I am reminded by email that my genealogical contact information has recently been added to the Madison County query list. Madison County is where Lizzie lived with Jeremiah and Arville in Plain City. As the saying goes, "Hope springs eternal."

Strange as it may seem, I'd rather not find her burial place. That would symbolize an end to her journey that I'm no longer willing to accept. Our family kept her secret too long. I know they buried her history to save her descendants from disgrace. I unbury her now hoping that beyond intolerance for the unworthy, there is a story here that is neither right nor wrong, it is simply Lizzie's story and if it was the truth, it should be known.

I may never find Lizzie's grave, but it would be impossible now, to bury her.

Lizzie on Scott and Addie France's porch photographed by Cleo New Philadelphia, Ohio 1918 [150]

Curtain Calls and Walk-Ons

I don't know the end of Lizzie's tale, but here are some back stories that relate:

Dayton's Enterprising Mrs. Hedges[151]

Lizzie's saloon and presumed "house" business didn't last long in Dayton. By late 1884, she had relocated to Marion, perhaps because the competition was keener in Dayton where another Liz – Mrs. Elizabeth 'Lib' Hedges – had already successfully established herself professionally starting as early as 1876. Lizzie Lape was a latecomer to the Dayton scene, while the buxom redhead Mrs. Hedges was already busy conquering the town. Lizzie's place at 16 East 6th was in direct competition with Mrs. Hedges' going concern on South Main Street in 1883.

By that date, Mrs. Hedges was starting to make capital improvements, expanding her operation from the back rooms of the South Main Street Saloon to the front parlors of several new homes she had built along Warren and Pearl Street. In fact, the whole length of Pearl Street with its flashy new red brick homes and festive glow-red windows – became an iconic location for many generations of Daytonians, with Lib Hedges running her operations there for over 39 years.

Dayton was known as one of the "cleanest towns", where the women of Pearl Street and other Dayton houses were registered and photographed by the police department, as well as checked annually for diseases which would prevent them from working in that city. During the hay-day in Dayton's Haymarket area, there were more than 150 women working and competing legally.

It was only when Dayton ended its legalized prostitution in 1915, that Mrs. Hedges gave up her profitable profession, joining the ranks of city benefactors. Daytonians did not soon forget Lib Hedges – her business prowess or her generosity of spirit to the women and men who worked for her. She was in point of fact, a credit to her profession.

Jeremiah 'Jerry' Lape – Lizzie's Husband # 1

Lizzie's ex-husband and Arville's named father died on September 8, 1890.

Photograph – courtesy William Fischer *Jr., Military Historian*[152]

His grave in Darby Township Cemetery, Plain City, Ohio, is mismarked with a later-day Spanish-American War service cross. The headstone does however, correctly identify his Civil War service with Company K, 54th Regt. Ohio Volunteer Infantry. He was a member of one of a number of Civil War Zouave units, distinguished by their colorful uniform which included a high profile fez with tassel, baggy trousers with white leggings, bold sash and short military jacket such as the one pictured here on Sergeant Lysander G. Huff of Plain City, Ohio, Jeremiah's fellow soldier and no doubt, friend.

Biography Collection of Plain City, Ohio, Library[153]

    The uniform had been popularized thirty years earlier during the North African and French wars. Poorly suited for North American climates and the practicalities of war, costumed Zouave units sustained higher than average casualty levels, due to their targetable characteristics.

Genetic DNA testing on Jeremiah's two brothers' descendants and Arville's descendants has provided no conclusive evidence that Lizzie's son, Arville, was Jeremiah's son.

George A. Huffman – Lizzie's Husband #2

History is no more alive than in this Curtain Call of George A. Huffman, Lizzie's partner in the Lima Junction House crime spree of prostitutes and thieves, circa 1885. With all other leads seemingly dried up, "George Huffman" and "Lizzie Lafe" returned to the stage in a December 30, 1885, Marion Daily Star newspaper appearance uncovered by a friend on the lookout for Lizzie. She found the article during the final editing stages of this book. With this new typographical error, a further web search on "Lafe" revealed a second earlier article of that same year.

"A family 'quarrel' among the dizzy dames and "Lord Chief Justice, Chief Solicitor, High Treasurer & c. & c.," of the Canal street bagnio caused the appearance of the entire crew at the Mayor's Court this morning. G. A. Huffman was fined for striking Dollie Day and the two were then ordered to leave town with the charming Lizzie Lafe. They will probably comply and Canal street will be rid of its greatest nuisance for a time at least."

Marion Daily Star – December 19, 1885

"Dollie Day and Lizzie Lafe, who had transferred their dive from Canal to Silver street when recently ordered to leave the city, were then pulled again last night and told to leave the city voluntarily or involuntarily. If they go by Saturday all will be lovely, but if not Mayor Gailey will forward them to the work house."

Marion Daily Star – December 30, 1885

It would take another 21 years for the 'charming' Lizzie Lape to voluntarily exit Marion, Ohio. But long before, probably between the first and second December 1885 Marion Daily Star articles, she had split from Huffman. Another article that came to light with the newly spelled Huffman web search, was a Sandusky Register 1889 announcement that George A. Huffman would be serving time in the Ohio pen for burglarizing the C. S. & C. railroad office in Sandusky. Hmmm. Guess we've heard that M.O. before.

John 'Jack' Larzelere – Lizzie's Husband #3

Jack Larzelere helped Lizzie run the "half-way" house of assignation owned by Jack "J. C." DeWitt in Bettes Corners between Akron and Cuyahoga Falls. After Lizzie divorced Larzelere in 1890, he remarried and moved north to Cleveland to run a saloon. On October 7, 1908, the *Elyria Telegraph* reported the headline, "Elyria Man Aids **Stabber's** Victim". Jack tried to stop two men caught exiting the flat above his saloon, when one of them **shot** him. Stabbed and/or shot, Jack survived and lived on until 1912, owning and operating his saloon located at the present-day entranceway to the Cleveland Indians Baseball Field.

Harry 'Snakes' DeWitt – Lizzie's Husband # 4

Lizzie divorced Harry DeWitt in 1891 in order to marry his father, Jack. Harry's *Akron Beacon Journal* 1909 obituary tells of Harry's death in Cleveland following an appendicitis operation, which was complicated by a gonorrheal infection according to his death certificate. His obituary mentions that he was a member of the I.A.T.S.E., the International Alliance of Theatrical Stage Employees. The theater seems to have touched many in Lizzie's life.

John C. 'J. C.'/'Jack' DeWitt – Lizzie's Husband # 5

Lizzie divorced Jack DeWitt in 1895 after three and a half years of wedded vice. Gentleman Jack left Akron and moved the operation to nearby Fairlawn's Croton Hotel. On July 19, 1898, the *Akron Beacon Journal* reported that Jack's horse-drawn wagon bolted, tipping the contents out and scattering the bottles "promiscuously" over the road. This sly reference to Jack's trade in more than liquor sales at the Croton, says it all for those in town who were in the know.

Jack lived another four and a half months, marrying a Miss Cora Ols on his deathbed. He had the pleasure of her company for nearly two weeks before succumbing to "paralysis". But his peace in death was short-lived. Another woman – Jennie Robinson – claiming to be his common-law wife, stepped forward to make a claim on his meager $500 estate. Even in death, Jack was being fought over by the ladies in his life.

He is probably buried alongside his first wife Mary and another son, William, in Mt. Peace Cemetery, however not one of his "ladies" saw fit to have the date marked on the DeWitt family monument. There were lots of unmarked graves in Lizzie's life.

Charles W. Veon – Lizzie's Husband # 6

Lizzie's marriage to Charles lasted five and a half years, ending in late 1900. Charles had a drinking problem before he married Lizzie which may have contributed to their break up. It also may have contributed to his "break in" of the Hibbard Jewelry Store on South Howard along with accomplice Tony Bauer in 1908. Charles blamed his predicament on imbibing too freely of liquor, and claimed he did not remember the heist.

Like Arville, Charles received the minimum one year sentence for his crime. But unlike Arville, Charles was sentenced to the Penitentiary in Columbus. His behavior in prison was very good, and he gained "trusty" status, allowing him more personal freedom there, than most inmates. He was released from prison after one year, and lived until 1929.

William B. Shetler – Lizzie's Husband #7

In 1940, Lizzie's youngest husband William B. Shetler died in Shelby. After his divorce from Lizzie in 1905, Bill made a real effort to pull his life together, marrying Lillian Hanna in Shelby, 1908. Two years later, Lillian died the day after Christmas 1910. Ten years later, according to the 1920 Sioux City, Iowa census, he was working and boarding near his brother James M. Shetler, a foreman at a tire factory.

But Bill returned to Shelby, sometime between 1920 and 1940 living out the remainder of his life just around the corner from the old Lewis House on North Broadway where Lizzie had run her restaurant and saloon alongside the B&O tracks.

John D. France, Lizzie's Husband #8

In 1923, J. D. married for the fourth time, a Mrs. Margaret Ann Powell White, but by the 1930 census he was listed as living in the Tuscarawas County Infirmary and died there in September. His obituary in the *Coshocton Times* said he was buried in Hollow Church Cemetery now Union Valley Cemetery in Dellroy, Carroll County, Ohio, alongside his first wife Mary E. Scott.

One son and two daughters were mentioned, unlike any of his four wives, including Lizzie. After his death, the France children maintained cordial relations with Cleo's family, sending a baby shower gift when Cleo's son, my father, was born.

Cliff Hanger in Stow Corners, Ohio

Frank Green, a Stow historian, wrote a story in 1942 for the Stow *Community Church News* titled "Stow's Stage Coach Tavern and the Township Lot On Which It Stood". It was sent to me by Fred Long, the current Stow historian, in response to my note of inquiry to Elizabeth Cowles, Frank Green's daughter and noted Stow historian. They welcomed and aided me. Making new friends such as these, has been one of the greatest gifts of this journey.

Excerpts from "Stow's Stage Coach Tavern and the Township Lot On Which It Stood", written in 1942 by Frank Green:

..."*The sentiment toward the use of intoxicating liquor gradually changed. When Stow was first settled there were comparatively few people who didn't drink some locally made whiskey. It could be bought for 25 cents a gallon. My Grandfather Green who was born in Ohio in 1811 and spent most of his life preaching told me that when he was a young fellow that he could drink his pint of grog and wheel a barrow up a plank with the best of them. Forty years later there were many people here in Stow who were strictly temperate and who realized the danger to the health and security of the neighborhood of such a place as the tavern. Of course this feeling was strongest among church members.*"

"*Oliver [Gross] had bought the land across the road [from the original tavern].*
He built the house north of Ada Marhofer's and continued to run a saloon and road house there for a long time. He called his place the Cliff House. The last proprietor of this place was Charles Kidney who was voted out of business when Stow adopted local option about 1884 or 5. Mr. Lane says that when Gross sold out, the tavern property was fenced in and was from then on private property."

"*During my lifetime here in Stow I have heard many tales about the people who frequented the Tavern. Many of them are unprintable. I came here to live in 1873, I was born in 1868. I have no recollection of the premises as they were when it was used for tavern purposes.... All this was in the misty past, but the history of Stow Tavern, in its later day, as it is recalled from the memory of those still living, is not attractive. All the stories I have ever heard about it tell of hard drinking and revelry. It was a loafing place for the men of the town and there was certainly to say the least nothing there to help them morally."*[154]

– Mr. Frank Green 1942

Lizzie's final ownership of Cliff House was not mentioned in Frank Green's bulletin. Odd, that. Was it chivalry on his part? Or perhaps the earlier generations of Stow residents didn't want to talk to their children about that incendiary fire. "Loafing place"... that would be Lizzie's.

Mansfield Ohio Reformatory – Haunted by the Living

Arville's great-grandchildren and great-great-grandchildren visited Mansfield Reformatory on Independence Day weekend 2009. Two hours was plenty of time for this great-granddaughter to take in the shocking sights, sounds, smells, and grim weight of incarceration that permeated it. We were overwhelmed just visiting.

The reformatory has experienced a whole new life recently, as a tourist attraction with the filming of *Shawshank Redemption* there in 1994. And many ghost hunters swear that the reformatory is haunted to a supernatural excess. It would be hard to imagine the ghost of happy-go-lucky Arville haunting this old hell hole.

Swan Song for a White Pigeon

When Lizzie's house of ill repute in Marion, Ohio, was under police siege in later years, this gentle article and poem about her place appeared on May 17, 1897, in the *Marion Daily Star*:

"A quaint author once wrote, 'Man born of woman is of few days and full schemes to get his name in the papers.' This is not always true. The pigeons who were recently disturbed in the west end by the police were full of schemes to keep their names out of the papers. The poet may have had the White Pigeon in mind when he wrote,

'There's the sound that rings over there...
A storm of wings in the forest wide;
The rising pigeons fill the air
Envelop the trees on every side
And –
The boughs with the widowed flocks have sailed,
The sweet sound of her wings are silent.'

But when Marshall Blain and his corps of officers finished their work things changed. The scene was lonesome. [155]

'The widowed pigeon, rocked on high,
Has cooed her last soft ode of love.'"

Warren Harding frequently wrote unsigned poetry for his own paper.
He would have remembered his old friend and outsider Lizzie, and happier days at the White Pigeon.

No man, father, brother, lover or husband can ruin my life.

I claim the right to live the life the good Lord gave me, myself.

- Florence Kling Harding

DEBRA LAPE • 247

Lizzie's 3 Generation Family

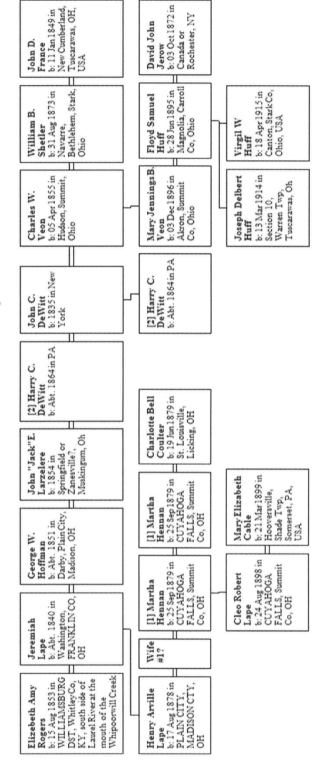

Lizzie's Trail

1853 – Whitley Co., Kentucky, birth

1860 – Williamsburg, Whitley Co., Kentucky, census

? – Chicago, Illinois, family oral tradition – "had a business there and marries her best customer"

1872 – Shelbyville, Shelby Co, Illinois, marries Jeremiah Lape

1880 – Pleasant Valley (now Plain City), Madison Co, Ohio, living with Jeremiah and son Henry Arville Lape

1882 – Fifth St. South of Naghten St., Columbus, Franklin Co, Ohio, city directory, boarding

1884 – 16 East 6th St., Dayton, Montgomery, Ohio, city directory, saloon operator

1885 – Lima, Ohio, arrest running Junction "house" and mention of earlier Wapakoneta robbery

1886 – Marion, Marion Co, buys the White Pigeon

1890 – Cuyahoga Falls, Summit Co, running a house with husband Larzelere

1890 – North Akron, Summit Co, lives at 113 Lods Ave with John C. DeWitt

1890 – Canton, Stark Co, marries Harry DeWitt

1891 – Akron, Summit, divorces son Harry, marries father John C. DeWitt

1895 – Akron, Summit, divorces John, marries Charles Veon

1896 – Stow, Summit, Lizzie's baby Mary born

1899 – Stow, Summit, Cliff House burns down

1899 – Marion, purchases another property in town, Lot 877 Wallace & Trues section.

1900 – Shelby, Richland, Ohio, buys Lewis House on North Broadway – a saloon and "house", divorces Charles later that year

1903 – Covington, Kenton, Kentucky, marries William Shetler

1904 – Marion, sells the White Pigeon

1906 – Shelby, lives at 1 Earl Ave. with Arville and Mary

1908 – North Fairfield and Norwalk, Huron Co, Ohio, marries John France and buys property in Greenfield Twp, Huron Co.

1910 – New Cumberland/Warren Twp, Tuscarawas Co, Ohio, census living with John France, daughter Mary Veon, and grandson Cleo Lape.

1918 – Late in year – New Cumberland/Warren Twp, Lizzie writing letters to grandson Cleo. Picture of "Grandma" taken by Cleo in New Philadelphia.

After 1918 – Where did she go?

November 2, 1920 – How would Lizzie have cast her first presidential vote?

I am still: Looking4Lizzie@gmail.com.

Acknowledgments

With heartfelt gratitude to those who have taken this journey into the past along with me, leading the way, sharing the experience, and making it a thrilling train ride:

- Wendy Raymont – for working tirelessly to bring order and clarity to Lizzie's story, and for suggesting I look for Warren G. Harding, too.
- Bob Lape, my dad, co-editor and attentive audience, for putting Lizzie on an editorial diet and coaching me throughout. I would not have wanted to do it without you, Dad.
- Perry Lackowski, my son – for editing, formatting, Lizzie's draft book cover, two bird cages and constant faith.
- Miranda Peters for designing Lizzie's book cover.
- Tim Page – Dawn Powell's biographer and keeper of her flame and my kind mentor. I looked for Lizzie and found Dawn, Carol & Sally, thanks to you.
- Carol Warstler – Dawn Powell's niece who shared her aunt Dawn's life stories which me, for which I am honored.
- Sally Maier of the Shelby Museum of History – for sharing your whole city plus a sandwich at a special Shelby saloon.
- Fred Long – for bringing Stow's naughty Cliff House back to life.
- Sherry Hall – curator and historian at the Warren G. Harding Home in Marion, Ohio, for reining me in, on my wildest suppositions.
- Jim Robenalt – author of "The Harding Affair", who let Harding do the talking.
- Charlotte May, Herb II and Herb III Lape, Mike Lape, Donna Wills, George Buckner and Kim Thurman – for being willing to admit that we share the same family tree.
- Marianne Szabo – Director of Publication Content for the Dallas Genealogical Society, for her sound advice and words of encouragement.
- The staffs of the Akron-Summit County Public Library, the Ohio Historical Society Archives and Library, the Marion County Historical

Society Museum, the Marvin Library in Shelby, Ohio, the Norwalk-Huron Co. Library, the Whitley County Kentucky Historical Society and Library and the hundreds of people I have written to over the years – thank you for keeping me in a continual state of amazement. If I have made mistakes in recreating Lizzie's life line, my hope is that you will continue to help me find, fix and thereby lead the way to more serendipitous discoveries!

- Countless County Courthouses and their staff who shared their treasures.
- The helpful staff members of the St. John's Episcopal Church of Cuyahoga Falls and Wesley M.E. Church (c/o Prospect St. United Methodist Church) in Marion, Ohio, who opened their doors wide for Lizzie and for me.
- My brother Bob Lape and husband Claude Lackowski for finding more "Lizzies" in those county record books than one could possibly imagine.
- My sister Alida Lape-Peters for being the first person to actually invest in a printed copy of the manuscript *Looking for Lizzie*.
- My brother Doug Lape for the beautiful oil painting of our great-grandmother, Martha 'Mattie' Atherholt.
- Grandma Mary Lape – for showing me the way to the Akron-Summit County Public Library and providing the first Lizzie clues.
- Authors Ted Gup and Karen Abbott – for telling the truth about our past, even when it was, Hard Times.
- Lizzie – for loving the same family I love.

Methodology

Researching Lizzie has been more of a personal odyssey than a purposeful search, beginning as early as the 1980's when I ordered a copy of Arville's Utica, Ohio, death certificate. Finding her has been a daisy chain of discovery, with one revelation leading to another, sometimes years apart. In July of 2008, I struck gold using the Ancestry.com online newspaper search. The *Marion Daily Star* was partially digitized, as were many other late 19th and early 20th century newspapers in North Central Ohio. The volume of references to Lizzie and the White Pigeon, as well as Arville and Mattie was extraordinary by contemporary standards of journalistic privacy. For its day, it was *not* unusual. Therefore, the recent digitization of these newspapers and periodicals has become a brand-new frontier for researchers of this era. Small town papers loved to feature their readership because it sold papers, as Editor Harding knew.

In early November 2008, I drafted the first chapter of Lizzie without knowing where it would lead. Life held many delays, but I really got engaged in writing her story in 2010, sending my father serial chapters as I made each new discovery which seemed to tumble out of my computer. I learned a great deal about Lizzie by studying her era and her contemporaries. As a genealogist, I worked to understand her choices in the context of her own time, enjoying every angle of the story. For example, I liked researching the history of a brass car journal, which Arville stole from the "Big Four". And, it was fun to figure out that the *Mushroon* sauce was not a typographical error on Lizzie's 1882 Thanksgiving Day "Dear Honey" menu, but in fact a perfectly legitimate and early French way of pronouncing the word circa 1882. I've thoroughly enjoyed talking to so many interesting people with their *own* family stories, to name a few:

- ➢ The great-grandson of the undertaker who buried Lizzie's last known husband J. D. France
- ➢ The great-grandson of Charles Veon
- ➢ The great-grandnephew of Warren G. Harding
- ➢ A Marion historian who grew up on its wild west-side and remembers that the White Pigeon was there at least until after WWII
- ➢ Gifted authors of some brilliantly illuminating books about the era
- ➢ My far-flung genealogical network of friends and family – all talented and gifted researchers who never stop giving and sharing

Lizzie's story could have been derailed a thousand ways – by me – and I've got lots of extraneous chapters drafted and deleted, to prove it.

My step-mother Joanna Pruess, a published author herself, was kind enough to look over my dad's shoulder and called me up one day to announce that I was in fact "writing a book" – news to me. That phone call was precisely what made me believe that I could and should continue to write Lizzie's story. Joanna was also responsible for introducing me to her close friend and gifted editor Wendy Raymont. Wendy is the reason this book is readable. Without her rearranging the chapters, Lizzie might have stayed in the order *I found* her, instead of the order in which she lived her life. I am eternally grateful to these women for guiding me.

Regarding my research methodology: I used *Family Tree Maker* software to organize the family genealogy, part of which is private offline; and much more of which can be found online. I found Lizzie through the generosity of others; I would like to return that favor.

My Lizzie filing system consisted of two key components. First was a digital file of newspaper clippings and digitized photographs. When I would see something Lizzie-related online, I would take a screen snapshot and save it to this folder, naming it chronologically with the format: year.month.day; then event; followed by source. The computer also saved the date I stored the item.

Ancestry.com and Google.com and Google News Archive specifically, are deep and constantly improving wells of genealogical information. When I visited a library or courthouse, I took digital photographs of documents. This was more efficient than photocopies. The quality was better and it saved wear and tear on the original document. I asked permission of librarians and record keepers to photograph the documents and almost unanimously they preferred this method, unless access to the documents was limited. I accumulated over 700 significant digital documents in this chronological folder. I used Google's free *Picasa* images software to sort and view this file, by file name or by date saved.

My second organizational component was a time line spreadsheet with column headers labeled with: Date of Event, Lizzie's age, Arville's age, Location, Event, and Source. This tool was invaluable to analyze what happened when and where. This led to many new ideas about where to look next for Lizzie. And, it was a great cross-reference for the clippings file.

One of the most rewarding parts of researching Lizzie has been the field trips to places she landed. It took online discoveries to get me out of the house and off to visit people and places where the trains took her. I sensed a story bigger than those hinted in the papers, and had to know more. Luckily, I live within driving distance of many of the North Central Ohio locations that Lizzie haunted, including Akron, Marion, Shelby, Norwalk, Stow, Newark, Canton, New Cumberland, Columbus, Lima, Plain City, Cuyahoga Falls, North Fairfield – all towns and cities that I've visited with my understanding husband Claude. Even Williamsburg, Whitley County, and Covington, Kentucky, and Chicago, Illinois, were planned stops on our family trips. Everyone knew what I was up to. To say that I was *thrilled* to visit these locations is an understatement.

What's more amazing is that I didn't have to look very hard to find plenty of places that Lizzie walked in all of these towns. If others could see what I saw in these byways, they would flock to see the origins of America, in the rough. They are authentic. They are the real deal. They are where we come from. Try Utica, Ohio's Watt's Restaurant; Canton's Bender's; Shelby's Weber's saloon; the Cumberland Falls of Kentucky; the gorge in Stow. Some wonderful things don't change.

And then, take a walk down the alley that abuts Lizzie's old White Pigeon lot, and watch two young boys hauling scrap metal away in a baby buggy. You blink and think, "Which one is named Arville?" Some things don't change but you wish they would. Then you pause in the alley dust and suddenly remember that Lizzie's and Arville's lives were *filled* with second chances, and you discover that beyond reason, you are hopeful.

On my journey to find Lizzie, I uncovered so much more than I bargained for.

My methodology is quite simple. I'll keep looking for her, because I am hopeful.

Bibliography and Source Notes

Books and Articles

Abbott, Karen. Sin in the Second City: Madams, Ministers, Playboys, and the Battle for America's Soul. 2008.

Adams, Samuel Hopkins. Incredible Era: The life and times of Warren Gamaliel Harding. 1939.

Adler, Polly. A House Is Not A Home. 1953.

Alderfer, Horace Freed. The Personality and Politics of Warren G. Harding. Syracuse University dissertation. 1929.

Anthony, Carl Sferrazza. Florence Harding: The First Lady, The Jazz Age, And The Death Of America's Most Scandalous President. 1999.

Asbury, Herbert. The Gangs of Chicago: An Informal History of the Chicago Underworld. 2002.

Baughman, A. J. History of Huron County Ohio – Its Progress and Development. 1909.

Britton, Nan. The President's Daughter. 1927.

Bryan, Mary Baird. The First Battle/Life of William Jennings Bryan. 1896.

Carson, Gerald. American Heritage Magazine "THE SALOON". 1963.

Chicago Vice Commission. The Social Evil in Chicago. 1911.

Commercial Law. 1895. Textbook.

Dean, John W. and Arthur M. Schlesinger. Warren G. Harding (The American Presidents Series). 2004.

Downes, Randolph C. The Rise of Warren Gamaliel Harding 1865 – 1920. 1970.

Ferres, J. Report of the Commissioners for Victoria Australia to His Excellency the Governor for the Philadelphia Exhibition of 1876. 1877.

Flahardy, Jason. Compiler. A Short Biography of Lexington's Most Famous Lady. University of Kentucky Libraries. Exploreuk.uky.edu.

Green, Frank. Stow's Stage Coach Tavern and The Township Lot On Which It Stood. Feb. 27, 1942.

Greiner, Marley. Canton Ohio's Red Light District. Thesis. Ohio State University.

Grismer, Karl H. History of Akron and Summit County. 1950.

Gup, Ted. A Secret Gift: How One Man's Kindness – and a Trove of Letters – Revealed the Hidden History of the Great Depression. 2010.

Hannum, Alberta Pierson. Look Back With Love: A Recollection of the Blue Ridge (mountains, VA, NC, WVa, KY, TN, GA, AL). 1969.

Jenkins, T. C., Superintendent. The Ohio State Reformatory, Mansfield Ohio, 1896 – 1934.

Kendall, Kathleen E. Communication in the Presidential Primaries: Candidates and the Media, 1912 – 2000. 2000.

Lane, Samuel. Fifty Years and Over of Akron & Summit County. 1892.

Laning, Jay Ford. Ohio Legal News, Volume 3. 1896.

The Marion Star. Publisher. Looking Back: Historical Images of Marion County, Ohio. 2003.

McClure Magazine – 1921 Retrospective Volume 53, p 21

"Anti-Saloon League Repudiates Bryan." New York Times. April 1918. Query.nytimes.com. Web.

Pancoast, S. The Ladies' New Medical Guide. 1892.

Parkhurst, Charles Henry. Municipal Reform Movements in the United States. 1895.

Powell, Dawn. Dance Night. 1930.

Powell, Dawn. Introduction by Tim Page. The Diaries of Dawn Powell 1931 – 1965. 1998.

Powell, Dawn. My Home is Far Away. 1944.

Robenalt, James D. The Harding Affair: Love and Espionage during the Great War. 2009.

Russell, Francis. The Shadow of Blooming Grove: Warren G. Harding in His Times. 1968.

Russell, Francis. The Shadow of Blooming Grove: Warren G. Harding in His Times. 1968.

– author's notes held at the University of Wyoming

Young, Roz. Mrs. Hedges' House. Montgomery County Historical Society. Dayton, Ohio. 1967.

Zacks, Richard. Island of Vice: Theodore Roosevelt's Doomed Quest to Clean Up Sin-Loving New York. 2012.

Maps

Combination Atlas Map of Summit County (1874)
Illustrated Summit County, Ohio, 1891; Akron Map & Atlas Company
Map of Pittsburgh, Marion, and Chicago Railway between Chewton, Penna. and Marion, Ohio and connections. (1887) (Library of Congress)
Sanborn Fire Insurance Maps; Sanborn Map Company
(Library of Congress)

Libraries and Historical Associations

Akron–Summit County Public Library and the Akron Beacon Journal Microfilm Index
Allen County Museum & Historical Society. Lima, Ohio.
Warren G. Harding Symposiums – 2011, 2012, 2013.
The Ohio State University. Sponsored Events.
Hervey Memorial Library – Licking County Library. Utica, Ohio.
Mansfield/Richland County Public Library. Mansfield, Ohio.
Marion Ohio Heritage Hall and Marion Historical Society.
Warren G. Harding Home, Marion, Ohio.
Wesley M.E. Church History Archives.
(c/o Prospect St. United Methodist Church, Marion, Ohio).
Newark Public Library. Newark, Ohio.
Norwalk-Huron County Library. Norwalk, Ohio.
Ohio Historical Newspapers including the Akron Beacon Journal, Akron Daily Democrat, Richwood Gazette, Shelby Times, Shelby Globe, Lima Daily Democratic Times, Mansfield, Daily Shield, Mansfield News, Marion Daily and Weekly Star, Utica Herald, Marysville Tribune, and others.
Ohio Historical Society Archives, Columbus, Ohio.
(Mansfield Reformatory records).
Ohio Historical Society Archives, Columbus, Ohio.
(Mansfield Reformatory records).
Plain City Public Library. Plain City, Ohio.
St. John's Episcopal Church, Cuyahoga Falls, Ohio.
Shelby Ohio – Marvin Library.
Shelby Ohio Museum of History.
Stow-Monroe Falls Public Library. Stow, Ohio.
Whitley County Historical Society, Williamsburg, Kentucky – www.wchgs.org

Whitley County Public Library, Williamsburg, Kentucky.

Websites – Historical and Research

www.Ci.akron.oh.us – History of Akron – Mayors.
www.SummitMemory.org
(administered by the Akron–Summit County Library)
www.Ancestry.com.
www.ChroniclingAmerica.loc.gov.
Library of Congress Historical Newspapers.
www.FamilySearch.org –
The Church of Jesus Christ of Latter-Day Saints.
www.Findagrave.com
www.Flickr.com
www.Google.com and Google News Archive Search Tool.
www.History.ky.gov – Kentucky Historical Society.
www.LOC.gov. Library of Congress Prints and Photographs Division Washington, D.C.
www.Mrps.org – The Mansfield Reformatory – history.
www.Minerd.com – Mineral City source.
www.SeeMidTN.com – Brent Moore.
www.Newspaperarchive.com.
www.OhioHistory.org and www.OhioHistoryCentral.org.
www.Legalgenealogist.com – Judy G. Russell.
www.Lib.utexas.edu – William Jennings Bryan –
University of Texas at Austin.
www.Wikipedia.org

Index

44th Ohio Infantry 26
54th Ohio Volunteer Infantry 34
Agate, Reverend Herbert 219
Akron Goodyear Wingfoot baseball team 14
Akron, Ohio 77
Akron's Music Hall 225
American Hotel in Columbus, Ohio 41
Anderson, 'Squire 92
Anthony, Susan B. 90
Anti-Saloon League 100
Atherholt, William 6
Barrett family 139
Battle of Camp Wild Cat 25
Battle of Shiloh, Tennessee 35
Bauer, Tony 239
Beckley, Sheriff Frank 73
Bettes Corners 109
Big Four 151, 168, 184, 253
Blain, Marshall 69, 70, 151, 244
Blue Goose 70
Boder's Market 109
Brezing, Belle 112
Brightman Mfg. Company 215
Bryan, William Jennings 55, 129
Buchtel College 140
Bunch, Madam 182
Burk, Nellie 148
Canton, Ohio 14, 79
Canton's Tenderloin 79
Chicago, Illinois 30, 33
Cliff House 20, 143
Columbus, Ohio 37
Company K, 54th Ohio Volunteer Infantry 34
Cornwell, Chief 207
Coulter, Lottie 213
Covington, Kentucky 197
Croton Hotel, Fairlawn, Ohio 238
Cumberland Falls, Whitley County, Kentucky 137
Cuyahoga Falls, Ohio 109
Dayton, Ohio 43, 233
DeWitt, Harry C 79, 81, 96, 237
DeWitt, John C. 77, 78, 79, 84, 89, 95, 98, 103, 106, 107, 108, 123, 238
DeWitt, Mrs. Mary C. 84
DeWitt, Solomon 96
DeWitt, William 96
DeWitt, William H. and Latisha ... 84
DeWolfe, Marshall 118
DeWolfe, Pete 118
DeWolfe, Simon 118
Dow, General Neal S. 99
Everleigh sisters 34, 113
Everleigh sisters, Minna and Ada 113
Fish Creek, Ohio 178
Ford, May 151
France, John D. 217, 218, 219, 221, 222, 230, 240
France, John D's children Scott and Catherine 221
France, Mrs. Mary B. Scott 221
France, Randall 217
France, Scott & Addie 232
Fritz, Dan 61, 67, 69, 70, 115, 119, 121, 123
Fritz, Dan and Martha 69, 141
Gaylord, 'Squire 162
Gompf, 'Squire 154

Good Citizenship League 118
Gorge House 20
Grant & Sieber 116
Green, Frank 241
Greenfield Twp., Huron County, Ohio 219
Greeno, George 207
Gregory, H. 73
Griffith, Mrs. Rebecca Rogers 24
Gross, General Oliver E. 20
H. W. Sager 72
Hammel's Business College in Akron, Ohio 126
Hanna, Lillian 240
Harding, Mrs. Florence Kling DeWolfe 58, 66, 246
Harding, Mrs. Phoebe 58
Harding, Warren G. 51, 53, 54, 55, 58, 59, 61, 62, 63, 66, 118, 148, 244
Hawks, Miss Carry 106
Hedges, Elizabeth 'Lib' 233
Heilman, Carrie 207
Hennan, Clarence 139
Hennan, Martha 'Mattie' 2, 3, 5, 7, 19, 134, 140
Hibbard Jewelry Store 239
Hill, H. Edmund 183
Hoffman, George 45, 50, 65, 79
Hope, Bob – aka Leslie T. Hope ... 188
Hoyles, Horatio 116
Huber Manufacturing Company . 194
Huber, Edward 194
Huber, John A. 199
Huber, John and Edward 206
Hudson, Charles and Columbus 26
Huff, Floyd 14
Huff, Sergeant Lysander G. 234
Huff, Virgil 14

Industrial School, better known as the B.I.S., was a well-known place of imprisonment in Lancaster, Ohio, for juvenile delinquents . 188
International Alliance of Theatrical Stage Employees 237
John Lust & Son Co 72
Johnson, B. W. 41
Kell, Reverend Robert 145
Kenzie, Margaret 207
Kidney, Charles and Elsie 139
Kling, Amos 59, 65, 66, 194
Lakeside Park at Summit Lake 107
Lang, George 162
Lang, Schenk & Co 72
Lape vs. Lape et al 73, 75
Lape, Cleo 5, 8, 13, 15, 161, 202, 216, 222, 225, 227
Lape, Edna 106
Lape, Henry Arville 5, 15, 19, 36, 49, 73, 75, 95, 98, 124, 127, 137, 150, 153, 154, 158, 170, 177, 178, 179, 181, 182, 184, 187, 189, 192, 199, 200, 223
Lape, Jeremiah 16, 34, 35, 36, 37, 38, 39, 73, 75, 95, 234
Lape, Mrs. Mary Ann 36
Lape, Mrs. Mary Cable 5, 6, 9
Lape, Zachariah 34, 36
Larkin Soap Company 225
Larzelere, John E. .. 65, 66, 67, 79, 237
Laurel River at the mouth of Whipperwill Creek 24
Leader Building 194
Leggett, Mrs. Mary Jane Baxter ... 221
Leisy Brewing Company 72
Levee, Chicago, Illinois 34
Lewis House 168, 169

Lewis, Jacob 168
Lima, Ohio 45
Lizzie Madison's sporting house . 171
Malleable Iron Works 115, 199
Mansfield Ohio Reformatory 187, 242
Marhofer, Ada 241
Marion Brewing & Bottling Company 72
Marion Department Co. 72
Marion, Ohio 50
Marquard, Mrs. L. 96
Masterson, Officer 69, 183, 184
May, Mrs. Charlotte Kent 36
McClung, Clark 43
McClure, W. H. 182
McEldowney, James 119
Merwin, George 223
Mineral City, Ohio 221
Monahan, Officer 69, 184
Monuett, Ohio Attorney General 100
Murphy, Officer 69, 153
New Cumberland, Ohio 14, 221
New Philadelphia, Ohio 230
New Republic berthed at Lakeside Park 104
New Shelby Inn 215
Newark, Ohio 216
North Fairfield, Ohio 220
North Hill, Akron, Ohio 109, 110
Norwalk Baptist Church 219
Norwalk, Ohio 217
Ols, Cora 238
Parkhurst, Dr. Charles H. 116
Patterson, Officer 184, 207
Plain City, Ohio 16
Powell, Dawn 170, 172
Powell, Mrs. Margaret Ann 240

Red Bird Saloon aka the White Pigeon 62
Robinson, Jennie 238
Rogers, James , a Revolutionary War veteran 23
Rogers, John 24
Rogers, Judith 24
Rogers, Lewis and Betsy 218
Rogers, Prior 23, 25
Rogers, Prior and Cynthia 26
Rogers, Prior and Cynthia's children First came oldest son J. W., then Lizzie, followed by Luke, Nancy who died in infancy, then youngest brothers Alex and Henry 26
Rogers, William 24
Roosevelt, Police Commissioner Teddy 116
Scofield, Levi T. 189
Scott, Colonel John S. – Second Cavalry Brigade of TN 26
Scott's Raid – Colonel John S. Scott 26
Sears, Will 26
Sexton, Mrs. Mary Polly Rogers .. 24, 35
Shannon, Alice 139, 141
Shannon, Robert O. 143
Shelby Seamless Tube Company 170, 200
Shelby, Ohio 168
Shelbyville, Illinois 34
Shetler, James M. 240
Shetler, William B. 197, 240
Shiloh, Tennessee 34
Sieber, Judge George W. 123
Silver Lake Amusement Park 225

Skiles, Skiles & Green 175, 179
Skiles, W. W. 175
Steinbacher, Jane 164
Steinbrueck, Mrs. Orpha Sherman
 169
Stinson, Mrs. Sally Rogers Stephenson 24
Stow Corners Hotel aka Cliff House aka Kidney Hotel *aka* Gorge House 163
Stow Corners, Ohio 19
Stow, Ohio 133
Sullivan, Mrs. Minnie Underwood
 225
The W. H. M. [Women's Home Mission] society of Wesley M. E. Church will meet at the home of Mrs. Charles Winfield 206
Thomas, Mrs. Almira Bigelow 36, 38
Thompson, Thomas A. and Isabella
 116
Timken Diner 14
Tuscarawas County, Ohio 221
Underwood, Mrs. Lilly Shannon 141, 145, 225
Underwood, Richard ... 161, 162, 164
Underwood, Richard & Lilly 141, 158, 175
Utica, Ohio 223
Vanderbilt, George W. 29
Vanderbilt, William H. 29
Vaughan, Colonel James 62, 63
Veon, Charles W. 108, 109, 145, 147, 153, 164, 173, 239
Veon, Mary Jennings Bryan 13, 131, 139, 145, 172, 182, 216, 223
Veon, Mrs. Ella 109
Veon, Robert 157
Veon, Robert & Ellen 139
Voris, Judge 106
Wapakoneta, Ohio 47
Warren Township, Tuscarawas County, Ohio 217
Watters, Lorenzo Dow 73, 75, 76, 83, 85, 95, 96, 119, 123, 127, 188, 191, 202
Weatherholt, Mattie 183
Weber's Bar, Shelby, Ohio 159
Weir bought the Pigeon for $5,500
 207
Wellington, Ohio 19
Wesley Home Missions Society ... 195
Wesley Methodist Episcopal [M.E.] Church 194, 195
White Dove 70
White Pigeon 57, 58, 61, 62, 63, 65, 67, 69, 70, 72, 73, 75, 76, 83, 84, 100, 115, 116, 120, 121, 122, 123, 141, 143, 147, 150, 151, 153, 154, 155, 157, 158, 167, 169, 175, 177, 181, 182, 183, 185, 192, 193, 194, 205, 207, 208, 215, 244, 253
Whitley County, Kentucky 16, 23, 39
Williamsburg, Kentucky 23
Winn, John W. 100
Yellow Canary 70

End Notes

[1] Author's family collection.

[2] Lape, Douglas C. 1987. Oil portrait of Great-Grandmother Martha Hennan Atherholt.

[3] Author's family collection.

[4] Author's family collection.

[5] Author's family collection.

[6] Arville Lape's Death Certificate. 1916. Ohio Historical Society. Columbus, Ohio.

[7] Lane, Samuel. 1892. *Fifty Years and Over of Akron & Summit County.*

[8] *Combination Atlas Map of Summit County.* 1874.

[9] Whitley County Will Book 1, p. 120-122 (book covers years 1818-1854), Whitley County Courthouse, Williamsburg, Kentucky.

[10] Image Online. Wolcott, Marion Post. 1940. *Kentucky River near Jackson, Kentucky.* Photographer for the U. S. Farm Services Administration - Library of Congress Prints and Photographs Division Washington, D.C., USA. Loc.gov. Web.

[11] Hannum, Alberta Pierson. 1969. *Look Back With Love: A Recollection of the Blue Ridge (mountains, VA, NC, WVa, KY, TN, GA, AL).*

[12] Image Online. U.S. Department of the Interior. *Cabin near Bell County, Kentucky.* 1946. Flickr.com. Web.

[13] Vanderbilt, William Henry. Chicago Daily News, October 9, 1882. Wikipedia.org. Web.

[14] Our American Cousin – the popular 1858 three-act farce starring actress Laura Keene at Ford's Theatre in Washington, D.C. on April 14, 1865 and attended by President Abraham Lincoln and his wife Mary during which he was assassinated by John Wilkes Booth.

[15] Author's note – Was it coincidence that Lizzie's nearest descendants informally enjoyed the stage – Arville with his Fraternal Order of Eagles Club extravaganzas, Cleo with his Green Room Club of the Goodyear Tire and Rubber Company Musical and Dramatic Productions, and my own father's little theater productions and distinguished broadcasting career? Acting was in the DNA.

[16] Image Online. *"The great fire in Chicago - panic-stricken citizens rushing past the Sherman House, carrying the aged, sick and helpless, and endeavoring to save family*

treasures". Frank Leslie's illustrated newspaper, vol. 33, no. 839 (1871 Oct. 28), pp. 104-105. Library of Congress – Prints and Photographics Division, Washington, D.C. USA. Loc.gov. Web.

[17] Asbury, Herbert. 2002. *The Gangs of Chicago: An Informal History of the Chicago Underworld.*

[18] According to Mary Cable Lape.

[19] "The prominent candidates for marshal at the next election are... [list follows including] ...Jerry Lape. "There are a few others; but they don't amount to much." – *Marysville Union County Journal, March 20, 1884.*

[20] Image Online. *Marysville Tribune, Wed. Sept. 17, 1890.* From the Library of Congress website Chronicling America: Historic American Newspapers. Chroniclingamerica.loc.gov Web.

[21] Asbury, Herbert. 2002. *The Gangs of Chicago: An Informal History of the Chicago Underworld.*

[22] Microfilm. *Lima Daily Democratic Times*, April 6, 1885. Lima Public Library. Lima, Ohio.

[23] *Marion Daily Star. April 23, 1886.* Marion, Ohio.

[24] *Marion Weekly Star. Dec. 24, 1886.* Marion, Ohio.

[25] *Marion Daily Star. Dec. 25, 1886.* Marion, Ohio.

[26] Image Online. Warren G. Harding image. 1882. Wikimedia.org. Web.

[27] Downes, Randolph C. 1970. *The Rise of Warren Gamaliel Harding 1865–1920.*
Excerpt quotation:
"Talk about Marion—Write about Marion—Be friendly to everybody—Sell all you can—Buy all you can at home—Support your town newspaper—Advertise."
Warren G. Harding, Marion Daily Star, May 16, 1887
Author's note – Harding was the driving force behind the turn-around success of the *Marion Daily Star*, not Florence his wife, according to his biographer Randolph C. Downes. Early in his editorial career he made lots of mistakes in his paper, alienating businessmen (such as his future father-in-law) and politicians alike. But by the time of his marriage to Florence Harding, he'd cut out the venomous politics and editorial infighting to a large extent, focusing on reporting the stories. An example:
"There is a rumor that there is to be a restoration of the Red mansion in the West End, not by the same Lizzie, old girl, but by Dan Fritz. The revival is the subject of some comment." – Marion Star. Nov. 20, 1890.

[28] Dean, John W. and Arthur M. Schlesinger. 2004. *Warren G. Harding (The American Presidents Series).*

[29] Reference: *Looking for Lizzie*, Postscript – *Swan Song For A White Pigeon.*

[30] Image Online. Sanborn Fire Insurance Maps; Sanborn Map Company. Library of Congress – Prints and Photographics Division, Washington, D.C. USA. Loc.gov.

[31] *Richwood Gazette. May 26, 1881.* Richwood, Ohio.

[32] Hotel Marion Menu. 1885. Star Job Printing House. Author's collection.

[33] Russell, Francis. 1968. *The Shadow of Blooming Grove: Warren G. Harding in His Times.*

[34] Anthony, Carl Sferrazza. 1999. *Florence Harding: The First Lady, The Jazz Age, And The Death Of America's Most Scandalous President.*

[35] *Marion Daily Star. Dec. 11, 1886.* Marion, Ohio.

[36] *Marion Daily Star. Feb 17, 1887.* Marion, Ohio.

[37] *Marion Daily Star. Feb 15, 1889.* Marion, Ohio.

[38] Weintraub, Joseph. 1967. *The Wit and Wisdom of Mae West.*

[39] *Akron Beacon Journal. May 31, 1890.* Akron, Ohio. Akron-Summit County Public Library.

[40] Microfilm. *Akron Beacon Journal.* Sept. 27, 1890. Akron, Ohio. Akron-Summit County Public Library.

[41] Adler, Polly. 1953. *A House Is Not A Home.*

[42] *Marion Daily Star - Sept. 23, 1892.* Marion, Ohio.

[43] Author's note – The "Lape vs. Lape et al" case was presented in Summit County and could not be located by the Court. Jeremiah Lape's name is not directly referenced in the Marion County trust for Arville Lape.

[44] Image Online. Lorenzo D. Watters. *History of Akron – Mayors.* Ci.akron.oh.us/history/mayors. Web.

[45] *1890-91 City Business Directory* for Akron. City Directories. Akron-Summit County Public Library. http://sc.akronlibrary.org/genealogy/city-directories/. Web.

[46] Ferres, J. 1877. *Report of the Commissioners for Victoria Australia to His Excellency the Governor for the Philadelphia Exhibition of 1876.* Google eBooks

[47] Greiner, Marley. Thesis on the Red Light District of Canton, Ohio – Ohio State University.

[48] Personal collection of Dr. Wayne B. Cook.

[49] *Akron Beacon Journal. March 19, 1891.* Akron, Ohio. Akron-Summit County Public Library.

[50] Microfilm. *Akron Beacon Journal. March 21, 1891.* Akron, Ohio. Akron-Summit County Public Library.

[51] Microfilm. *Akron Beacon Journal. August 25, 1891.* Akron, Ohio. Akron-Summit County Public Library.

[52] Marriage License of J. C. DeWitt & Lizzie Rogers. Dec. 8, 1891. Summit County Marriage Book. County Court House, Akron, Ohio.

[53] Image Online. North Howard Street, Akron, Ohio. *General Photograph Collection.* Permission of the Akron-Summit County Public Library. *SummitMemory.org.*

[54] Microfilm. *Akron Beacon Journal. Nov. 10, 1891.* Akron, Ohio. Akron-Summit County Public Library.

[55] Microfilm. *Akron Beacon Journal. November 11, 1891.* Akron, Ohio. Akron-Summit County Public Library.

[56] [Henry O.] Arville Lape's Guardianship Records. 1891-1895. Summit County Court House, Akron, Ohio.

[57] Grismer, Karl H. 1950. *History of Akron and Summit County.*

[58] Carson, Gerald. 1963. *The Saloon.* American Heritage Magazine. 1963, Vol. 14, Issue 3. Americanheritage.com. Web.

[59] *Temperance Movement.* Ohio History Central. Ohiohistorycentral.org. Web.

[60] Laning, Jay Ford. 1896. *Ohio Legal News*, Volume 3. Google eBooks.

[61] Image Online. *Akron City Directory (Burch)* Advertisement. 1894. Akron, Ohio. Akron-Summit County Public Library.

[62] Chicago Vice Commission. 1911. *The Social Evil in Chicago.* Archive.org. Web.

[63] Microfilm. *Akron Beacon Journal. July 17, 1894.* Akron, Ohio. Akron-Summit County Public Library.

[64] Microfilm. *Akron Beacon Journal. April 13, 1895.* Akron, Ohio. Akron-Summit County Public Library.

[65] Image Online. *Akron City Directory (Burch)* Advertisement. 1894. Akron, Ohio. Akron-Summit County Public Library.

[66] Photograph of *North Howard Street (& North Hill), Akron Ohio 1902.* From the collection of the Akron-Summit County Library – Special Collections.

[67] Flahardy, Jason. Compiler. *A Short Biography of Lexington's Most Famous Lady.* University of Kentucky Libraries. Exploreuk.uky.edu. Web.

[68] Abbott, Karen. 2008. *Sin in the Second City: Madams, Ministers, Playboys, and the Battle for America's Soul.*

[69] Online Photograph of Belle Brezing. 1895. Wikipedia.org. Web.

[70] *Marion Daily Star. July 16, 1895.* Marion, Ohio.

[71] *Marion Daily Star. December 10, 1895.* Marion, Ohio.

[72] Zacks, Richard. 2012. *Island of Vice: Theodore Roosevelt's Doomed Quest to Clean Up Sin-Loving New York.*
[73] *Marion Daily Star. August 6, 1895.* Marion, Ohio.
[74] Parkhurst, Charles Henry. 1895. *Municipal Reform Movements in the United States.*
[75] *Marion Daily Star. September 7, 1895.* Marion, Ohio.
[76] *Marion Daily Star. September 7, 1895.* Marion, Ohio.
[77] *Commercial Law.* 1895. Textbook from Hammel's Business College. Akron, Ohio. – author's family collection.
[78] *Illustrated Summit County, Ohio.* 1891. Akron Map & Atlas Co.
[79] Photograph of *Doyle Block* on Howard Street, Akron Ohio. Before 1892. From the collection of the Akron-Summit County Library – Special Collections.
[80] Author's family collection.
[81] Photograph of William Jennings Bryan. Wikipedia.org. Web.
[82] Bryan, Mary Baird. 1896. *The First Battle/Life of William Jennings Bryan.* En.wikisource.org. Web.
[83] Kendall, Kathleen E. 2000. *Communication in the Presidential Primaries: Candidates and the Media, 1912 – 2000.* (Westport, CT: Praeger Publishers).
[84] In the late summer of 1896, William Jennings Bryan spent many days and weeks in Ohio. His speech locations read like the a train ticket through mid-Ohio – Ada, Alliance, Bucyrus, Canton, Massillon, Crestline, Lima, Mansfield, Upper Sandusky on 8/10; Shelby, Galion, Gilead 9/1, Kenton 9/2, Wapakoneta, Lima 10/19… and on October 20th he stopped to speak in Ravenna, Kent and Akron. In Kent there was a crowd of 2,000 people waiting for him at the depot. (As gleaned from almost as many local Ohio newspapers heralding his arrival).
[85] "Anti-Saloon League Repudiates Bryan." New York Times. April 1918. Query.nytimes.com. Web.
[86] *Combination Atlas Map of Summit County.* 1874.
[87] *Combination Atlas Map of Summit County.* 1874.
[88] Author's family collection.
[89] Author's family collection.
[90] Author's family collection.
[91] Image from *Marion Daily Star - May 4, 1897*. Marion Public Library. Marion, Ohio.
[92] *Map of Pittsburgh, Marion, and Chicago Railway between Chewton, Penna. and Marion, Ohio and connections.* 1887. Library of Congress – Prints and Photographics Division, Washington, D.C. USA. Loc.gov. Web.

[93] *Marion Daily Star. Oct. 2, 1897.* Marion, Ohio.
[94] *Marion Daily Star. Nov. 18, 1897.* Marion, Ohio.
[95] *Marion Daily Star. Dec. 6, 1897.* Marion, Ohio.
[96] Carson, Gerald. 1963. *The Saloon.* American Heritage Magazine. 1963, Vol. 14, Issue 3 excerpt:
"There was always a brewer or distiller ready to put up the cost of the license fee if he could only get another outlet operating. Thus developed the abuses of the "tied house." Pushed by promissory notes, mortgages, the need for ever greater volume, the saloonkeepers in this unhappy condition could survive only by breaking the law. They purchased votes, stuffed ballot boxes, rigged elections, shielded criminals, sold liquor to minors and hopeless winos. On those rare occasions when a publican was hauled off in the meat wagon, an alderman would very often appear in police court and say, "Your Honor, I've known this boy for years. He's a good boy an' works hard an' takes care of his ole mother." Since the alderman would very possibly have helped to seat the magistrate on the bench, the beetle-browed "boy" would be quickly released." – Gerald Carson.
[97] Microfilm. *Akron Beacon Journal. Aug. 20, 1898.* Akron, Ohio. Akron-Summit County Public Library.
[98] *Akron Beacon Journal. October 6, 1898.* Akron, Ohio. Akron-Summit County Public Library.
[99] Image Online. *Akron Daily Democrat. May 27, 1899.* From the Library of Congress website Chronicling America: Historic American Newspapers. Chroniclingamerica.loc.gov Web.
[100] Microfilm. *Akron Beacon Journal. Sept. 7, 1899.* Akron, Ohio. Akron-Summit County Public Library.
[101] Green, Frank. 1942. *"Stow's Stage Coach Tavern and The Township Lot On Which It Stood."* Stow-Monroe Falls Public Library. Stow, Ohio.
[102] *Akron Daily Democrat. Oct. 30, 1899.* From the Library of Congress website Chronicling America: Historic American Newspapers. Chroniclingamerica.loc.gov Web.
[103] *Akron Daily Democrat. Oct. 28, 1899.* From the Library of Congress website Chronicling America: Historic American Newspapers. Chroniclingamerica.loc.gov Web.
[104] Microfilm. *Mansfield News.* "Brief News Notes [from Shelby, Ohio]". January 1, 1900. Mansfield/Richland County Public Library.
[105] Powell, Dawn. 1944. *My Home is Far Away.*
[106] Powell, Dawn. 1931 – 1965. Introduction by biographer Tim Page. 1998. *The Diaries of Dawn Powell 1931 – 1965.*
[107] Powell, Dawn. 1930. *Dance Night.*

[108] Microfilm. *Mansfield News and Shelby Times.* April 27, 1900. Mansfield/Richland County Public Library.

[109] Microfilm. *Akron Beacon Journal.* July 31, 1900. Akron, Ohio. Akron-Summit County Public Library.

[110] Image Online. *Akron Daily Democrat.* July 31, 1900. From the Library of Congress website Chronicling America: Historic American Newspapers. Chroniclingamerica.loc.gov Web.

[111] Image Online. *Akron Daily Democrat.* Aug. 1, 1900. From the Library of Congress website Chronicling America: Historic American Newspapers. Chroniclingamerica.loc.gov Web.

[112] Image Online. *Akron Daily Democrat.* Aug. 9, 1900. From the Library of Congress website Chronicling America: Historic American Newspapers. Chroniclingamerica.loc.gov Web.

[113] Image Online. *Akron Daily Democrat.* Aug. 11, 1900. From the Library of Congress website Chronicling America: Historic American Newspapers. Chroniclingamerica.loc.gov Web.

[114] *Akron Beacon Journal.* Dec. 7, 1900. Akron, Ohio. Akron-Summit County Public Library.

[115] *Marion Daily Star.* Aug. 3, 1901. Marion, Ohio.

[116] Microfilm. *Mansfield News and Shelby Times.* Aug. 11, 1901. Mansfield/Richland County Public Library.

[117] *Looking Back: Historical Images of Marion County, Ohio.* 2003. Marion Star.

[118] *Marion Daily Star.* Nov. 9, 1901. Marion, Ohio.

[119] *Marion Daily Star.* Feb. 6, 1902. Marion, Ohio.

[120] *Marion Daily Star.* Feb. 19, 1902. Marion, Ohio.

[121] Jenkins, T.C., Superintendent. 1934. *The Ohio State Reformatory, Mansfield Ohio, 1896 – 1934.*

[122] Image Online. *Akron Daily Democrat.* Feb. 1, 1902. From the Library of Congress website Chronicling America: Historic American Newspapers. Chroniclingamerica.loc.gov Web.

[123] Mansfield Reformatory Photographs of Arville Lape. 1902. Ohio Historical Society Archives. Columbus, Ohio.

[124] Image from *Marion Daily Star.* Dec. 18, 1901. Marion Public Library. Marion, Ohio.

[125] *Marion Daily Star,* May 12, 1887. Marion, Ohio.

[126] Image Online. Wesley M.E. Church History (c/o Prospect St. United

Methodist Church, Marion, Ohio).

[127] *Marion Daily Star. Jan. 26, 1903.* Marion, Ohio.

[128] Image Online. Photographer: Shahn, Ben. "Untitled. Steam Thresher. These machines moved from job to job under their own power." 1938. From the Library of Congress website Chronicling America: Historic American Newspapers. Chroniclingamerica.loc.gov Web.

[129] Photograph of *Shelby Tube Steel Workers. Annealing Night Gang.* 1902. The Shelby Museum of History, Shelby, Ohio.

[130] Mansfield Reformatory Record of Arville Lape. 1902. Ohio Historical Society Archives. Columbus, Ohio.

[131] Both Arville and Mattie had suffered at the hands of their parents. Both were orphans with living parents. Both intended to protect their son Cleo from their own past mistakes. And both succeeded. To my knowledge my grandfather never knew that his father served time.

[132] Author's family collection.

[133] Image from *The Mansfield Daily Shield. March 6, 1903. The Shelby Globe. March 2, 1903.* Mansfield / Richland County Public Library. Mansfield, Ohio.

[134] *Marion Daily Star. Mar. 17, 1903.* Marion, Ohio.

[135] *Marion Daily Star. Aug. 5, 1903.* Marion, Ohio.

[136] *Marion Daily Star. Mar. 17, 1906.* Marion, Ohio.

[137] *Marion Daily Star. Jun. 15, 1906.* Marion, Ohio.

[138] Microfilm. *Mansfield News. Sept. 9, 1905.* Mansfield/Richland County Public Library.

[139] Microfilm. *Mansfield Daily Shield. Oct. 30, 1905.* Mansfield/Richland County Public Library.

[140] *Akron Beacon Journal,* January 22, 1906

[141] Microfilm. *Mansfield Daily Shield. Mar. 17, 1906.* Mansfield/Richland County Public Library.

[142] Microfilm. *Mansfield Daily Shield. Jul. 5, 1907.* Mansfield/Richland County Public Library.

[143] Author's family collection.

[144] Image Online. Marriage Record. Huron County, Ohio. *The Church of Jesus Christ of Latter-Day Saints.* Familysearch.org. Web.

[145] Marriage Record. May 19, 1908. Huron County Courthouse. Norwalk, Ohio.

[146] Peters, Miranda. Photo graphic of North Fairfield, Ohio, building.

[147] Author's family collection.

[148] *Akron Beacon Journal* movie ad for *The Shepherd of the Hills. April 1917.* Akron-Summit County Public Library.

[149] Author's family collection.

[150] Author's family collection.

[151] Young. Roz. 1967. *Mrs. Hedges' House.* (Dayton, Ohio). Montgomery County Historical Society.

[152] Fischer, William. Jeremiah Lape – grave photo – by Retired Major William Fischer, Jr., U.S. Air Force, National Park Service Historian, who voluntarily photographed hundreds of Civil War soldiers' gravesites in Ohio, contributing to FindAGrave.com.

[153] Lysander G. Huff Genealogy. Biographical Collection. Plain City Public Library. Plain City, Ohio.

[154] Green, Frank. Feb. 27, 1942. *"Stow's Stage Coach Tavern and The Township Lot On Which It Stood.* Stow-Monroe Falls Public Library. Stow, Ohio.

[155] *Marion Daily Star. May 17, 1897.* Marion, Ohio.

About the Author

Debra Lape is a business graduate of Cleveland State University and controller at TES Engineering, an engineering consulting firm in Cleveland, Ohio. Her 40-year quest to discover the secret life of her great-great-grandmother was two parts amateur genealogy and one part pure obsession. An Akron, Ohio, native, she and her husband Claude and son Perry live in Westlake, Ohio.

Made in the USA
San Bernardino, CA
02 March 2014